Preventing Workplace Violence From Infiltrating Business

Markeith L Porter

MS, University of Phoenix, 2006

BS, University of Phoenix, 2004

Copyright © 2015 Markeith L Porter
All rights reserved.

ISBN: 1503239004
ISBN 13: 9781503239005
Library of Congress Control Number: 2015900031
CreateSpace Independent Publishing Platform
North Charleston, South Carolina

Abstract

Preventing Workplace Violence From Infiltrating Business

MarKeith Porter

MS, University of Phoenix, 2006
BS, University of Phoenix, 2004

December 2014

Abstract

The low rate of businesses that have policies to address externally generated workplace violence is significant in the US Southwest. Based on Zammuto et al.'s contingency theory, the purpose of this qualitative case study was to explore and identify strategies to protect companies against liability claims filed by victims of externally generated workplace violence. The research question involved identifying what strategies could prevent externally generated workplace violence from infiltrating organizations. Data analysis was performed by using semistructured interview questions to help me explore how strategies could prevent externally generated workplace violence from infiltrating the organizations to reduce litigation, ensuring the policy addressed the major themes of awareness, procedures, safety, security, and definition. The findings help frontline managers operate more effectively when incidents of externally generated workplace violence arise. Implications for social change include adopting internal strategies that include policies and procedures aimed to address externally generated workplace violence and safeguards to increase the leader's situational awareness, which is a concern for employees and the community. The results of this study might contribute to social change by increasing managerial awareness of externally generated workplace violence in business, thereby increasing workplace safety, reducing costs, and preventing liability issues.

I dedicate this study to the business professionals who have experienced workplace violence and thought that no one cared. My mother was a victim of externally generated workplace violence. I also dedicate this to my mother, Betty Francis, who taught me to love humanity in general; my grandmother Marion Hall, who taught me to be proud; Mr. Richard, who taught me hard work; my wife, Irma Porter; my children, Markeith J. and Sabrina Porter; my grandson, Markeith K. Porter; my sisters, Sandra Wood, Linda Porter, Marion Edwards, and Karen Washington; my brother, John Smiley; my son's wife, Emily Porter and my brother-in-law Armonda Tafoya who teaches me every day to be humble.

Acknowledgments

I would like to give a special thanks to Dr. Kenneth Gossett. It was special for me to be under your mentorship. From my family to yours, thank you.

Contents

List of Tables xvii
List of Figures..xix
Section One: Foundation of the Study................................1
Background of the Problem 3
Problem Statement 4
Purpose Statement 4
Nature of the Study 5
Research Question..7
    Subquestions 7
    Interview Questions 7
Conceptual Framework 9
Definition of Terms 10
Assumptions, Limitations, and Delimitations 12
    Assumptions 12
    Limitations 13
    Delimitations 13
Significance of the Study 14
    Contribution to Business Practice 14
    Implications for Social Change 14
A Review of the Professional and Academic Literature 16
    Conceptual Theory 17
    Women and Violence 18
    Men and Violence 19
    Violence and Liability 21
    Employer Workplace Strategies................................ 23
    Violence Services Programs..................................... 24

Medical Costs and Violence	25
Violence Mitigation Strategies	27
Court Cases and Violence	42
Transition and Summary	43
Section Two: The Project	45
Purpose Statement	45
Role of the Researcher	46
Participants	46
Research Method and Design	48
Method	48
Research Design	49
Population and Sampling	51
Population	51
Sampling	51
Ethical Research	53
Data Collection	54
Instruments	54
Data Collection Technique	55
Data Organization Techniques	56
Data Analysis Technique	57
Research Subquestions	57
Interview Questions.	58
Reliability and Validity	60
Reliability	60
Validity	62
Transition and Summary	62
Section Three: Application to Professional Practice and Implications for Change	64
Overview of Study	64
Presentation of the Findings	66

Research Subquestion One 66
Research Subquestion Two 68
Research Subquestion Three 69
Research Subquestion Four 69
Applications to Professional Practice 70
Implications for Social Change 70
Recommendations for Action 71
Recommendations for Further Study 71
Reflections 71
Summary and Study Conclusions 72
References 75
Appendix A: Consent Form 95
Appendix B: Subquestions and Interview Questions 97
    Subquestions 97
    Interview Questions 97
Appendix C: Case Study Protocol 99
Curriculum Vitae 101

List of Tables

Table 1. A Sample Table Showing Correct Case

List of Figures

Figure 1. Figure caption, sentence case

Section One: Foundation of the Study

Two million employees suffer from violence in the workplace each year (Keelty 2013). Four hundred and fifty-eight fatalities occurred in the workplace in 2011 (Keelty). Intimate partner violence accounted for 12.7 percent of these violent incidents. The incidents include simple assault, harassment, and rape. Externally generated workplace violence can take many forms and occur with regularity (Howard and Wech 2012). Most employers do not maintain formal externally generated workplace violence policies (Keelty 2013).

Externally generated workplace violence (EGWV) takes many forms. Workplace violence (WPV) is an illicit behavior or action that reduces the actual or perceived security of employees, patrons, and leaders (Howard and Wech 2012). WPV might occur at company events outside of regular working hours where employees gather for work-related social events, meetings, or team-building exercises (Howard and Wech 2012). A limited number of investigators focused their research on EGWV incidents (Howard and Wech 2012). For the purpose of this research, externally generated workplace violence may include instances in which the perpetrator has no legitimate relationship to the business, yet threatens or assaults an intended victim while at work or off duty. The relationship between the perpetrator and victim might include a family member, boyfriend, or spouse (Lindquist et al. 2010). The problem of intimate partner violence that infiltrates the workplace is a growing concern for organizations in the United States.

Company managers do not show that externally generated workplace violence is an issue until the problem becomes significant. Training and funding from the US Department of Justice might serve to limit the problem of violence in the workplace. Pollet (2005) suggested that whereas some employers are addressing the issue by focusing on employees, others are not, making the problem difficult to manage (Stark 2010).

The problem of externally generated workplace violence is pervasive. WPV can occur in a number of ways, and women are often the victims. Ueno and Kamibeppu (2011) found that a husband or boyfriend physically or sexually abused 31 percent of American women at some point in their lives. More than one million people in the United States report a violent assault by an intimate partner every year (Devries et al. 2013). Most victims of violence affect the workplace in the form of being late or missing work (Al-Modallal et al. 2012). Approximately 37 percent of women who experienced externally generated workplace violence reported that the abuse had an effect on their performance by making them late, miss work, lose a job, or lose a promotion (Hobday 2010). Hobday (2010) reported that some women who have experienced violence are in poor health, suffer from depression, or both, which likely negatively affects job performance. Fifty-five percent of executives stated their company's financial performance would benefit from addressing the issue of externally generated workplace violence among their employees (Hobday 2010). Domestically abused employees were less likely to be absent from work after receiving counseling (Katula 2012). Kitterlin (2010) noted that abused employees' absenteeism rates returned to the rates of nonabused employees after receiving counseling.

Externally generated workplace violence has implications for the victim's job performance and for his or her safety while at work because abusers may stalk or hurt someone in the business environment. Ninety-four percent of corporate security directors indicated that externally generated workplace violence is a high-security concern. Employers that fail to protect their employees from violence at work put the organization at risk for litigation (Hartley, Renner, and Mackel 2013). Juries have awarded victims average settlements of $600,000 because of inadequate security (Pollet 2005).

Violence has implications for the perpetrators and the victims of externally generated workplace violence. Managers can fire or lay off victims for the disruption the violence causes to the workforce. Employees who require time off and leave work early often cause management to punish the victim (Katula 2012). Depending on the severity of abuse, workers can lose a day or up to a week of work. The organization's productivity suffers when employees miss work. Managers play a fundamental role in implementing organizational policies to control issues relating to externally generated workplace violence.

Background of the Problem

Corporate employees who experience the effects of externally generated workplace violence understand that externally generated workplace violence does not happen in a closed environment and the abuse poses adverse consequences to victims. Approximately,75 percent of victims face harassment from intimate partners while at work (Futures Without Violence 2014). Ninety-six percent of assaulted women who work experience problems at work because of the abuse suffered at home (American Institute on Domestic Violence 2014). Victims of externally generated workplace violence are less productive, are absent and late more frequently, and are more prone to job loss than employees not affected by abuse. Externally generated workplace violence causes legal issues for businesses; for example, the perpetrator might follow or attack his or her partner or other people working in the organization. Abuse can occur between dating or married coworkers. Workplace policies and procedures would enable management to deal with the result of an externally generated workplace violence incident and perhaps prevent future incidents. Educating managers and employees about externally generated workplace violence would benefit society and the workplace.

Problem Statement

More than one million people are victims of violent crimes in the United States. Twenty percent of the assaults occur from externally generated workplace violence, and more than seven hundred result in workplace homicides annually (Keelty 2013). Businesses incur a loss of $3 billion to $5 billion in expenses attributable to absenteeism, lower productivity, higher turnover, and health and safety costs associated with externally generated workplace violence each year (Hobday 2010). The general business problem is that leaders must implement proactive strategies that shield employees from and address the effects of externally generated workplace violence to avoid costly litigation. The specific business problem is that some leaders might have limited knowledge to safeguard organizations against liability claims filed by victims of externally generated workplace violence.

Purpose Statement

The purpose of this qualitative, exploratory, single-case study is to identify strategies to protect companies against liability claims filed by victims of externally generated workplace violence. A qualitative, exploratory, single-case study is best for exploring the perceptions of managers who supervise victims of violence (Denzin and Lincoln 2011; Yin 2009). The business under exploration is located in the coastal region of the US Southwest. Semistructured interview questions from the sample of twelve managers will illustrate strategies aimed to guard against potential litigation resulting from the manager's negligence to shield victims of violence. The results of this study might contribute to social change by increasing managerial awareness of externally generated workplace violence in business, thereby increasing workplace safety, reducing costs, and preventing liability issues for business owners (Lim and Tai 2014).

Nature of the Study

In this qualitative, single-case study, twelve managers working in a company in the coastal region of the US Southwest provided information on strategies aimed to guard organizations against liability claims resulting from incidents rising from victims of externally generated workplace violence. Wisdom et al.. (2012) described qualitative, quantitative, and mixed-method research strategies of inquiry. Quantitative methods of investigation show experimental or nonexperimental results of trends, attitudes, and opinions of the population using surveys to test one or more null hypotheses (Rubin and Rubin 2012). A quantitative method is not appropriate for this research because a statistical representation would not illuminate the participant's unique experiences regarding the topic under exploration. Quantitative research requires focusing on the examination of relationships among variables and the testing of theories and hypotheses (Denzin and Lincoln 2011; Gephart 2004).

Gephart (2004) and Yin (2009) noted that qualitative researchers apply interviews, documents, and field notes to gather rich data to explore one or more phenomena. I chose a qualitative research method because the managers participating in this research could describe his or her strategy used to safeguard employers against liability claims from incidents of externally generated workplace violence. The participants in this study might show underlying issues rather than symptoms of a much larger problem. Broeder and Donze (2010) noted that qualitative researchers tend to assume that each participant brings a unique perspective to the study.

A mixed-method approach draws on both strategies of inquiry. The additional time and cost constraints preclude a mixed-method technique as a viable means for completing the study (Bernard 2013).

I selected a single-case study design to gather information regarding the experiences and perceptions of managers regarding their policies and processes for addressing externally generated workplace violence. A case study design allows participants to provide an in-depth account of their experience, which could help prevent or reduce liability issues and concerns for business leaders. A case study design is best suited for exploring the problem through the lens of one or more cases within a bounded system (Ashley 2012: Yin 2009).

A phenomenological approach is not appropriate for this research because the essence of human experience, such as an earthquake or natural disaster in which participants share the same experience, is not the topic of exploration. Similarly, the narrative design is also not feasible because a narrative approach allows researchers to gather data from observing participants in their natural setting; this will allow the informants to share their experience over a long period, much like the historic perspective.

Research Question

The central question for this research is the following: What strategies could prevent externally generated workplace violence from infiltrating the organization? Semistructured interview questions (see Appendix B) show the different strategies leaders adopt to reduce litigation that could result from managers who do not shield employees from externally generated workplace violence. The data could help stakeholders understand what factors influence positive organizational change relating to externally generated workplace violence.

Subquestions

The following research subquestions and interview questions will help guide the study:

1. What protocols and policies are implemented for the prevention, intervention, and dealing with the aftermath of violence that infiltrates the workplace?
2. What training are managers and employees provided about externally generated workplace violence?
3. How could leaders create an environment that supports victims and allows these individuals to report potential danger that could potentially infiltrate the workplace?
4. How could managers create an environment in which perpetrators know that violence is not acceptable behavior (on or off the job), and what community resources are available to offer help in changing behavior?

Interview Questions

1. How long have you been working as a manager in business?
2. How did you construct your policy to manage the issue of externally generated workplace violence?

3. How effective is the current policy and training on externally generated workplace violence?
4. How could regulations or laws help to manage externally generated workplace violence in business?
5. How could multidisciplinary teams (MT) perform in dealing with externally generated workplace violence?
6. What roles do each member of the MT play in dealing with externally generated workplace violence issues?
7. What training do supervisors and employees receive about how to respond to suspected externally generated workplace violence?
8. What symptoms are associated with externally generated workplace violence prior to an incident occurring?
9. What intervention and prevention measures are implemented for you as a manager?
10. What procedures and processes are implemented that demonstrate a climate of zero tolerance?
11. What other aspects could you offer about your company's current policies to prevent and address externally generated workplace violence?

Conceptual Framework

Zammuto et al.'s (2007) contingency theory is a conceptual framework proposed for this study. Contingency theory illustrates broad generalities of differentiating technologies. Zammuto et al. postulated that the technology affected (a) span of control, (b) centralization of authority, (c) formalization of rules, and (d) procedures. Contingency theory showed no single way to organize data to include mission statements and policies regarding an issue like externally generated workplace violence, and different ways of organizing the workforce are not equally effective (Valdiserri and Wilson 2010). Developing an effective externally generated workplace violence policy requires an organized effort to address the needs of managers so they gain experience in handling cases of externally generated workplace violence.

Lorsch (2010) described the basic components of contingency theory. Essential aspects to contingency theory are (a) organizations are open systems in need of management to fulfill and stabilize core needs, (b) management will help employees adapt to environmental conditions, and (c) no best practices exist for organizing information across companies (Lorsch 2010). The type of duty or environment in which an employee is working determines the appropriate contingency process. Effective leadership occurs when frontline supervisors provide suggestions on strategies to increase situational awareness of externally generated workplace violence (Al-Omari, Johari, and Choo 2012). The reactions from supervisors could satisfy and balance the internal statutory and legal requirements needed to safeguard employees and to protect the company's stockholders from incurring losses from liability and negligence damages.

Definition of Terms

Research-based definitions will assist the reader in understanding the phenomenon of externally generated workplace violence, which is the purpose of this research.

Adult protective services: Social services provided to abused, neglected, or exploited older adults and adults with significant disabilities (Cramer and Brady 2013).

Amenity providers: Amenity providers offer safe, accessible, and appropriate services that prevent domestic and family violence in the community, and support and empower people affected by domestic and family violence (Macy and Goodbourn 2012).

Civil protection order: A court-ordered legal intervention in which a person who harasses, threatens, or stalks another person must stop, with the goal of reducing the risk of further threat or harm to the person experiencing harassment (Tuerkheimer 2013).

Coercive control: A method of control used in domestic violence cases to control the victim. The method could be verbal, such as screaming, or physical, such as slapping (Colvin, Cullen, and Ven 2002).

Domestic violence: A situation in which individuals commit abusive behaviors in marriage, family, dating, friendships, or cohabitation relationships. This violence can come in different forms, such as kicking, shoving, hitting, slapping, or restraining (US Department of Justice 2012).

Domestic violence in the workplace: A situation in which an intimate partner's behavior interferes with an employee's ability to perform duties at work (Lindquist et al. 2010).

Domestic violence program: A program that provides help for women and children who consider moving rather than remaining in an abusive situation (Cramer and Brady 2013).

Duluth program: A program created to deal with domestic violence perpetrators by arresting the offender upon discovering the perpetrator in a hostile condition in the home (Corporate Alliance to End Partner Violence 2012).

Employee assistance program (EAP): A company-sponsored support and assistance program that provides help with work-related issues. A successful EAP must provide the following: expertise, advice, and resources and training (Sagor 2012; Virginia Department of Health 2013).

Externally generated workplace violence: A perpetrator who has no legitimate relationship to the business, yet threatens or assaults an intended victim while at work or on duty. The relationship between the perpetrator and victim can include a family member, boyfriend, or spouse (Lindquist et al. 2010).

Group work: A form of cooperative learning to reflect individual differences and develop students' knowledge (Livingston 2012).

Hyper arousal: A reaction given by the victim in response to previous assaults (Gotlib and Joormann, 2010).

Intervention: A control group that joins forces to break the cycle of destructive behaviors (Lindquist et al. 2010).

Motivational interviewing: A collaborative, person-centered form of guidance used to elicit and strengthen motivation for change (Zalmanowitz et al. 2013).

Multidisciplinary team: A team of official collaborators in a business designed to control domestic violence issues. The team is comprised of legal, EAP, safety, security, and environmental staff or consultants who address domestic violence (Virginia Department of Health 2013).

Perceived Consequences of Domestic Violence Questionnaire (PCDVQ): A survey used to assess the penalties of the intimate partner's violence as understood by the offender (Walker et al. 2010).

Perpetrator: A person who commits a crime or evil act (Colvin, Cullen, and Ven 2002).

Post-separation stalking: After a break in a relationship, a potential perpetrator desiring unwanted contact with the victim (Nelson 2012).

Responsible choices for men: A counseling group created to work with abusive men (Zalmanowitz et al. 2013).

Revictimization: A subsequent act of victimization that occurs after the initial occurrence (Iverson et al. 2013).

Trauma-focused cognitive behavioral therapy (TF-CBT): A child and parent psychotherapy approach for children and adolescents experiencing significant emotional and behavioral difficulties related to traumatic life events (Puccia et al. 2012).

Victim: A person suffering from an injury or death because of the perpetrator's wrongful action (Nichols 2011).

Assumptions, Limitations, and Delimitations

The theoretical lens recognizing the assumptions, limitations, and delimitations concerning this research follows. The justification will inform the reader of the constructs of this study under exploration (Yin 2009). The path began by evaluating the potential bias of conducting this study in a setting familiar to me, determining the appropriate sample size to achieve data saturation, and identifying the bounds of the study.

Assumptions

The ability to gather data in an impartial and fair manner from managers is my first assumption. Participants are current employees working in business in the coastal region of the US Southwest. Participants will provide honest and truthful answers to the interview questions. The information obtained from the respondents will allow me to address the research question proposed in the study.

Limitations

The failure to generalize the findings to other areas within the United States is a limitation of the proposed research (Marshall and Rossman 2011). Seidman (2006) suggested that qualitative researchers could acquire ample participants and achieve data saturation using the purposeful sampling method. I intend to reach data saturation following the direction of Francis et al. (2012), which will involve eight initial interviews, with a stopping criterion of two interviews devoid of new concepts rising. Member checking and triangulation will assist me to assure the validity of my study's findings. Triangulation of the data (Denzin and Lincoln 2011) include: (a) field observations, (b) workplace documents, and (c) semistructured interviews to support conclusions drawn from participants' interviews. The final limitation of the proposed study is that opinions of the participants may represent only the perceptions of frontline managers. Views from other stakeholders could reveal different perspectives regarding the presence, type, and effectiveness for workplace strategies that could improve externally generated workplace violence awareness.

Delimitations

The study location, that is, the coastal region of the US Southwest, the proposed business problem, and the sample size of twelve participants (Stake 2010) could restrict my exploration of the proposed research. Some business leaders have limited knowledge to safeguard organizations against liability claims resulting from incidents in which managers do not shield employees from externally generated workplace violence. I will explore the perceptions of business leaders to gather information to increase managerial awareness to combat the problem of such violence in the work environment.

Significance of the Study

Contributions to the business practice and understanding the implications for social change require strong leadership. Exploration of the participants' experiences and organizational structures could influence administrative and legislative responses to the problem of externally generated workplace violence. Following is a discussion of the significance of this proposed study.

Contribution to Business Practice

Exploring the forces and frameworks that promote or inhibit responses to the problem of externally generated workplace violence reveal strategies that could protect companies in the coastal region of the US Southwest against liability claims from employees. Participants could illustrate strategies aimed to guard against potential litigation resulting from the manager's negligence to shield victims of such violence in the workplace. Implementing an externally generated workplace violence policy, which includes incidents that infiltrate the organization, could include a training component, which would reduce the liability and negligence claims against business and increase the safety of employees. The findings might show cost savings from a reduction of violent activity.

Implications for Social Change

Leaders must consider the costs of violence in the workplace, including the affliction of human suffering. Victims of externally generated workplace violence suffer from both emotional and physical damage, which can affect their employment and personal life. Expenses plaguing the industry could force organizational leaders to adopt workforce violence policies, which address violent invasions, by creating responses designed to mitigate the financial costs associated with the problem. The leaders of the business could establish social change by adopting internal policies and procedures that address externally generated workplace violence, and putting safeguards in place to increase the leader's situational awareness, which is a concern for employees and the community. The results of this study might contribute to social change by increasing managerial awareness of externally generated workplace violence in business, thereby increasing workplace safety, reducing costs, and preventing liability issues for business owners (Lim and Tai 2014).

A Review of the Professional and Academic Literature

This review will help frame the problem in this study and offer an objective review of externally generated workplace violence. The intent of this study is to identify strategies to protect companies. Business leaders currently have inadequate information about how to safeguard a company from claims resulting from incidents in which managers do not shield employees from externally generated workplace violence. The purpose of constructing this literature review is to strengthen the conceptual framework and to explore concepts and assumptions posited by past theorists. The review of the literature begins with an overview of externally generated workplace violence and then looks at the history, similarities, and differences of the externally generated workplace violence programs. I will also cover the consequences of externally generated workplace violence, a description of the current responses to the problem, an assessment of the efficacy of violence mitigation strategies, and a summary of the underlying causes and motivations for externally generated workplace violence.

Literature for the study includes (a) peer-reviewed and other scholarly journal articles, (b) published dissertations, (c) books, and (d) government documents. I used records from online databases available through the CALUMS University Library, from specific databases including (a) ProQuest Central, (b) ScienceDirect, (c) Emerald Management Journals, (d) Sage Journals, and (e) LexisNexis Academic to substantiate the currency of abuse and ongoing efforts to combat the problem of externally generated workplace violence. Works from Google Scholar showed the importance to the literature review with identified articles subsequently obtained from CALUMS University Library databases. The Google search engine identified the titles of government documents of importance to the study topic. Government records were retrieved from the appropriate government websites (e.g., the US Department of Justice and US Government Accountability Office). The information drawn from peer-reviewed journals adds to the rigor of this study, while associated statistics reveal the magnitude of the problem of externally generated workplace violence. The remaining publications included peer-reviewed references outside of five years, books, government websites, or published dissertations. Keyword searches included *domestic abuse, violence in workplace, organizational determinants of violence,* and *externally generated workplace violence.*

Conceptual Theory

The purpose of this proposed qualitative, single-case study is to identify strategies to safeguard employers against liability claims filed by victims of externally generated workplace violence. Valdiserri and Wilson (2010) determined the best course of action is dependent on organizing information according to internal and external circumstances. Zammuto et al. (2007) postulated that technology affected (a) span of control, (b) centralization of authority, (c) formalization of rules, and (d) policies and procedures. Contingency theory showed no single way to organize data to include mission statements and policies regarding externally generated workplace violence; different ways of organizing the workforce are not equally effective.

In this study, the conceptual theory applied to externally generated workplace violence is the open systems theory. Externally generated workplace violence interacts with the environment dynamically. Dynamic systems in business evolve and change in response to system feedback (Bertanlanffy 1956). Running a business provides a framework for change. In this study, change is viewed as a dynamic response to violence. Externally generated workplace violence is limited in scope to the amount of change required to meet a business need.

Practices on how best to deal with externally generated workplace violence are forever shifting. As I view the open systems theory, I discuss tools for thinking about change and explanations of general patterns and obstacles (Bertanlanffy 1956). When business managers proceed with rigid ideas on how change should occur, most find that the dynamic, ever-changing circumstances of dealing with externally generated workplace violence are not sufficient. The feedback from a dynamic situation makes decision making at the manager level more precise to the given circumstance. For instance, a company may benefit from the open systems theory by meeting cultural changes and needs, allowing a company to assist employees and meet their specific needs. Thanks to social awareness, companies want to do business with a company that observes certain safety or environmental protocols. The corporate design is more advantageous and more socially conscious (Bertanlanffy 1956).

Women and Violence

Two-thirds of women in the workplace experience violence (Potter and Banyard 2011). Participants in this study found significant effects of violence against women on victims' work productivity and performance (Pollack, Austin, and Grisso 2010). The effects of violence are naturally complex and costly to organizations and society. Victimization occurs among women in middle- and high-income brackets (Kwesiga et al. 2007). These women reported the complex intersection of multiple forms of victimizations of women in the workforce (Banyard, Eckstein, and Moynihan 2010).

Potter and Banyard (2011) showed victims who had a low socioeconomic status worked fewer hours and weeks per year and were most likely to lose a job. Women employed in executive-level positions and received higher wages are not immune to violence (Kwesiga et al. 2007). Prevailing statistics highlight violence against women from differing socioeconomic groups. Komro, O'Mara, and Wagenaar (2012) reported that organizations could have a protective effect. Pollet (2005) found that 25 percent to 50 percent of victims lost their jobs because of violence. Economic abuse is a form of violence (Pollet 2005). Many abusers use the legal system to further contact and harass their victims by initiating extensive litigation, including filing repeated, frivolous, or unnecessary lawsuits. Forty-two percent of violent victimizations infiltrating the workforce file claims with law enforcement agencies (Renner and Stephen 2010). Violence associated with several problems can affect more than the victims' productivity.

The connection between violence and work is complex (Crowne et al. 2010). Crowne et al. (2010) found that women experience interfering tactics by abusive partners, including undermining efforts to get to work by hiding keys, not providing transportation funds, or not providing help with daycare for children (Swanberg, Logan, and Macke 2006). Violence is a contributing factor to victims' increased tardiness, absenteeism, and use of sick days. Violence also surfaces in the form of injuries and problems with concentration, work performance, and productivity (Hanson et al. 2010; Swanberg et al. 2006).

Men and Violence

Research and community efforts arose to develop effective support and intervention strategies for victims of violence and their children (Whitaker et al. 2013). Preventive and intervening crusades surfaced to encourage change in how the public responds to the problem of externally generated workplace violence. An effort to deter further assaults and understand how to approach and help perpetrators is underway. Perpetrators of violence typically receive assistance mandated by the courts through intervention programs after the offender commits an assault, yet many crimes go unreported. Perpetrators must obtain the help and support necessary to control their violent behaviors (Schenck-Gustafsson et al. 2012). Mdanda (2010) found that profeminist organizations, social service agencies, and battered women shelters have operated abuse programs. Agencies and churches that provide help to individuals joined with probation departments to work with inmates in penitentiaries and prisons. The majority of the programs (63 percent) are self-supporting and not part of a parent association, with 43 percent being private and nonprofit organizations, whereas 48 percent are private for-profit entities (Mdanda 2010). Activists had some success in changing policy and views in relation to fathers, families, and violence. Some advocates led campaigns to show that women equally abuse men. Activists shared information designed to raise awareness about violence against women to inspire a change.

Casey and Smith (2010) found that a participant's knowledge about sexual assault prevention programs are linked with the member's awareness of the issue of violence against women. Three recognizable themes emerged from the small number of studies that have shown factors associated with men's involvement in antiviolence or gender-equality efforts. Exposure to cases of assault or violence, or one's personal experience, is critical to understanding victims (Wies and Coy 2013). Receiving support or reassurance from peers, role models, and most important, female mentors initiated antiviolence efforts (Casey and Ohler 2011). The objective theme of peer-support findings demonstrated men's willingness to intervene in sexist peer behavior or situations that might lead to violence against women (Banyard et al. 2010). Longer periods of devotion to antiviolence efforts are necessary, including employing a social justice awareness of violence, which includes matters of racism and homophobia, and links violence against women to sexism (Carmody 2013).

Violence and Liability

Economic security is one of the most important factors a victim who wants to separate from an abusive partner must consider, but violence often interferes with the victim's ability to maintain a job, thereby further trapping her or him in an abusive relationship. Widiss (2008) found that organizations that support victims give credence to addressing violence as a liability issue. The empowerment of victims to take legal action bolsters other strategies for combating violence. Widiss (2008) identified major types of services among twenty-six private-sector companies that offered at least some violence-preventions:

- Policies addressing violence-response procedures followed by employees and managers, and procedures regarding protective orders.
- Security measures designed to prevent violence in the workplace and provide additional protection to employees identified as violence victims.
- Victim resources (e.g., providing paid time off, legal help, and referrals to community resources).
- Educational activities (e.g., trainings and other activities designed to educate employees about the company's antiviolence policy and increase the knowledge of signs of potential victimization and available resources).

The Occupational Safety and Health Administration has not distributed externally generated workplace violence standards, so employers do have an obligation to protect employees under the General Duty Clause enacted in 1970. The General Duty Clause states that every employer "shall furnish to each of his employees employment and a place of employment free from recognized hazards that might cause or are likely to cause death or serious physical harm to his employees" (p. 2). Externally generated workplace violence that infiltrates a workplace is an issue that needs addressing with academic rigor because the duty to protect is not common knowledge.

Statistics from the Bureau of Justice showed that 11,613 people were killed between 1992 and 2006 because of incidents of externally generated workplace violence. Employees sued for negligence if someone was aware of a dangerous situation and an incident of externally generated workplace violence subsequently occurred. Lawsuits showed that organizations were negligent in hiring, retaining, training, or supervising employees who went on to commit violence in the workplace. Employer liability does not represent the enormous liability associated with employee negligence. Incidents merely emphasize the point that to do nothing is not an adequate defense in mitigating violence that infiltrates the organization.

In *Lacey v. Village of Palatine* (2009), claims were brought against personnel, alleging negligence to defend two victims of violence who were killed after the employer received word of a man's decision to engage in a murder-for-hire plot. According to the plaintiffs, the man displayed an ongoing and regular pattern of abuse while residing with a woman who gained a protective order against him. Reports showed the perpetrator inquired about killing a woman. The complaint alleged that the failure to protect the woman and another family member (killed at the same time) violated the Illinois Violence Act. The court also ruled that because the second murder victim did not have her name on the protective order, she was unprotected by the statute.

In *Moore v. Green* (2006), a police officer failed to properly respond to a 911 call about domestic violence. The court decided that the police officer was negligent because he caused the woman's death when her husband subsequently shot her. The police officer failed to break into the woman's house because he did not want to incur a charge for damaging personal property. The court found that a police officer has a special duty to protect, especially when a person has a protective order in their possession.

The Montana Supreme Court issued a judgment against a sheriff for $358,000 for failure to protect and ruled the sheriff had a special duty to protect the victim from any prospective perpetrator. In this case, the sheriff had responded to the couple's violent incidents for more than three years but failed to inform the woman of available community resources (*Massee v. Thompson* 2004).

Employer Workplace Strategies

The Corporate Alliance to End Partner Violence found leaders in large corporations recommended their managers create programs to raise awareness of violence programs. One approach is to organize a multidisciplinary team. A multidisciplinary team should seek approval of upper management to engae the victim. The team should consist of people knowledgeable about security, the legal system, human resources, employee assistance, and community outreach (Puccia et al. 2012). The Corporate Alliance to End Partner Violence also recommends establishing a policy. A sound policy for externally generated workplace violence should be specific to this discussion. Policies could list symptoms of violence and use strategies such as flexible working hours, paid time off, and alternative work schedules to help employees become secure (Corporate Alliance to End Partner Violence 2012). The policy should provide training and ongoing education. Security officers must be knowledgeable to assess potential risks and know the warning signs to mitigate potential problems infiltrating the business. This concept could help those in positions offering community outreach (Corporate Alliance to End Partner Violence 2012). The company should be able to assist employees with employer resources and excellent community resources. These efforts only strengthen an employee's desire to report incidents (Corporate Alliance to End Partner Violence 2012). These steps pave the way for a comprehensive corporate policy and set the stage for a reduction in the incidents of violence. The Duluth model is one such approach.

Violence Services Programs

Violence services programs have remained under scrutiny after some predators made significant changes in their lives because of the help received from individuals involved in the programs (Sullivan 2011). Donors to these programs expect the nonprofit organizations to show responsible spending and demonstrate positive results for the service users. Mburia-Mwalili et al. (2010) observed that women who have suffered violence also show signs of depression, but social support protects women from depression. The results would not generalize to the general population because many abused women prefer not to seek out medical attention or violence-related services (Sohani et al. 2013).

The research finding of Nurius et al.(2011) demonstrated an association between survivors' appraisals of violence and employees' biopsychosocial needs, coping efforts, and willingness to seek help. Nurius, Logan-Greene, and Green, (2012) anticipated that higher vulnerability appraisals could stimulate a survivor's outreach to formal service providers. The relationship between vulnerability and seeking help would show in the presence of positive social support if survivors could accept informal sources of help.

Victims believe that programs designed for perpetrators do not reduce recidivism (Labriola, O'Sullivan, and Rempel 2010). Some offenders show only borderline improvements when given alternative penalties such as probation, community service, or court monitoring. Sixty-four percent of the judges offered a reduced sentence to defendants who completed a service program prior to ruling. Those who completed the program obtained legal benefits, such as removal of charges, lessening of charges, and decrease of sentence upon conviction.

The criminal justice system helps victims in the prevention of abuse (Tuerkheimer 2013). Strategies for seeking help vary, such as contacting the police, filing a petition for a protective order, filing criminal charges, seeking assistance from legal aid, testifying against the perpetrator in court, and providing testimony in a disposition. Women report that legal strategies are more helpful than efforts to manage abuse by pacifying and fighting the perpetrator. Multiagency partnerships developed as part of a political process to establish policies and improve local accountability (Harvie and Manzi 2011).

Medical Costs and Violence

Violence-related costs totaled $5.8 billion in the United States in 2009 (Kwako et al. 2010). Violence is associated with undesired results, including higher rates of emotional disturbances, such as posttraumatic stress disorder (PTSD), depression, and anxiety disorders (Aupperle et al. 2012). Those illnesses also include physical problems, such as increased morbidity and mortality, chronic pain, higher levels of sexually transmitted infections, fatigue, sleep disorders, and poor health (Cerulli et al. 2012). About 30 percent of females who report violence experience some physical assault to the head, neck, and face (Dennison and Thompson, 2011; Wu, Huff, and Bhandari 2010). Approximately 50 percent of the violence includes strangulation injuries (Campbell et al. 2010). Women who experience violence have an increased risk of developing PTSD symptoms, hyperactive arousal, and depressive symptoms (Gotlib, and Joormann 2010). Scholars have advocated the screening of violence against women in healthcare facilities to understand the extent, nature, consequences, risk, triggering factors, and potential barriers to intervention (Ballan and Freyer 2012). Other scholars found that wounds range in severity from bruises to fractured bones (Dalal, Andrews, and Dawad 2012) and some form of psychological illness, manifested in depression, anxiety, and PTSD (Rothman et al. 2011). Female victims of violence take on other problems, such as unhealthy diets, substance abuse, alcoholism, and suicide (Rothman et al. 2011). Rothman's research further indicates that women of reproductive age encounter reproductive health problems. Women often terminate pregnancy, miscarry, and have more undesired pregnancy than do peers in nonviolent relationships (Moore, Frohwirtha, and Miller 2010).

Access to healthcare services is a major concern for women afflicted with violence. Female patients were considerably more likely to access emergency services via 911 calls than were nonvictims (Resnicoff 2012). This recognition could potentially lead to initial interventions and prevention of further injury, threat, or harm to the victim if appropriate follow-up action does not take place. Hellmuth et al. (2013) reported that women develop PTSD after experiencing violence. Similarly, Wong et al. (2010) found mental health consequences of violence associated with increased occurrence of suicide and suicidal attempts. Cerulli and Edwardsen et al. (2010) found that women enrolled in a health maintenance organization were likely to possess a job. The same women reported higher wages than the national average and had experienced violence at a 6.1 percent rate in the prior year. Kelly (2010) found woman present more physical and psychological signs compared to their male counterparts. These injuries range from acute injuries, hypertension, gastrointestinal issues, genitourinary problems, chronic pain, depression, anxiety, and PTSD. These women need to use the healthcare system to help address these problems (Kelly 2010). Physicians noted that woman still experience trauma after the violence ends (Campbell et al. 2010). In the United States, evidence indicated that women who had experienced violence were at a significantly higher risk for stroke (Centers for Disease Control and Prevention 2011). The investigators in this study also identified an extensive health gap in the delivery of services to this population.

Violence Mitigation Strategies

Community leaders have been instrumental in forming a collective professional response to dealing with externally generated workplace violence based on conflict and control issues. Groups such as the (a) criminal justice system, (b) educators, (c) policy makers, (d) perpetrator treatment providers, and (e) legislators have led the response to externally generated workplace violence. The shelter systems stopped male violence by holding perpetrators fully accountable (Curwood et al. 2011).

A reduction of externally generated workplace violence involves a dedicated systemic approach, which includes development of policies and procedures; effective communication, training, and enforcement; and on-going effort to analyze and evaluate the workplace environment (Dillona 2012). If an organization's culture tolerates or encourages aggression, change will require commitment to a sustained cultural transformation effort. Cultural change would require outside assistance and could require the replacement of leadership unwilling to change. Employees in those organizations that ignore warning signs and only prepare for crisis management are at the greatest risk for externally generated workplace violence to occur (Dillona 2012). Employers should consider the potential risks of litigation and implement strategies to control violence infiltrating the organization.

Typologies of externally generated workplace violence show the conceptual model of continuum conflict and control research was identified (Carlson and Dayle 2010). The design features groups identified by typological members. Rooted in the continuum of conflict and control, training tools for couples counselors help dispel the notion that most forms of relationship violence are established through power and control issues (Carlson and Dayle 2010). The model could help couples counselors identify signs and symptoms of violence within relationships. Counselors could make decisions on appropriate treatment and interventions after assessing the type of violence. Counselors could also make recommendations for the welfare of clients (Carlson and Dayle 2010).

Many legislators in the United States developed feminist antiviolence methods that rely overwhelmingly on the criminal legal system without considering its biases, especially against people of color, undocumented immigrants, and poor communities (Abraham 2010). Abraham highlighted the ways in which such methods could fall short on the delivery of justice regarding policy formulation, practice, offender accountability, and addressing the victim's needs and safety. Neither partner has received much scholarly attention about a cessation of violence in their relationships, despite well-documented details in the research literature that outline the characteristics of both victims and perpetrators (Bonham and Vetere 2012).

Group work is expected to demonstrate national occupational standards for social workers. The climate of group work makes statutory social work synonymous with risk and care management (Livingston 2012). According to Dai (2013), the trend of group work in respect to welfare state retrenchment has reduced state expenditures for social services. Such organizations need to cultivate a supportive emotional culture that fosters solidarity and commitment. Feminist activists should either engage in a more open discussion about dependence and autonomy or pursue a strategy of organizing for state support.

In the context of coercive control, Brown (2012) described the limited effectiveness of perpetrator programs and identified factors that could improve those programs. The rejection-abuse cycle identifies a pattern of perpetrator behavior that links threats to self-rejection, abuse, and defense against the threat. The aforementioned patterns approach violence in a particular manner, and each helps reduce incidents of violence in its own way. Kulkarni, Bell, and Rhodes (2012) identified workplace factors associated with secondary traumatic stress. A sample of violence advocates working in diverse settings indicated that coworker support and quality clinical supervision are critical to the emotional well-being of advocates. An environment in which power, respect for diversity, mutuality, and consensually shared decision making is important. When these factors are present, some advocates provide better protection for victims than do more traditional, hierarchical organizational models. Shared power emerged as a workplace variable to predict traumatic stress beyond individual factors.

Violence has negative consequences on victims' employment (Swanberg, Ojai, and Macke 2012). Employers lag in recognizing this fact (Swanberg, Ojai, and Macke 2012). Some states such as California and Massachusetts have established that the public sector's response to violence is a workplace issue. Content analyses of 369 victim responses were used to form a state-level employment security policy for externally generated workplace violence victims. The summation of the results showed three broad policy categories: (a) policies that aim to reduce employment discrimination of externally generated workplace violence victims; (b) policies that offer work leave for victims, and (c) policies that aim to increase awareness and safety in the workplace (Swanberg, Ojai, and Macke 2012). Female victims of violence face serious career development challenges that necessitate the intervention and assistance of human resources (Collins 2011). Collins identified significant factors that had an influence on the career development of women and offered suggestions for how human resources practitioners could help women in the development of their careers.

Social developers and service providers described externally generated workplace violence as a social change movement (Nichols 2011). Even with concerns about the evolution of the movement into a political service provision, some studies have showed the status of the movement as a social change movement. Nichols examined the degree to which externally generated workplace violence advocacy was characterized as a social change movement. Nichols highlighted movement leaders' visions for a previously established movement. Nichols pointed to an action shift from the role of social service provider to a larger social change agenda. Suneetha and Nagaraj (2010) pointed to the resources women need to mobilize the family and community to realize their rights against violence. Suneetha and Nagaraj suggested that the institutionalization of this power has led women to become subject to a governmental mode of control, and the deployment of this power in everyday activism is more of a political goal than a guarantee of protection against violence.

Feminist politics has struggled to make visible an entire range of social practices. These unfriendly social practices are summed up under the term of *violence* (Suri 2011). Sen (2010) examined the legal rhetoric engaged with violence that women within marriage face. The three parts to this study featured (a) analysis of legal documents that describe physical violence; (b) exploration of the Protection of Women that through legal language makes a formal provision on translating suffering; and (c) how violence is understood by the women's movement.

Established interpersonal violence rather than sociology underscored several tensions, which have broader implications than health or legally defined behaviors (Hearn 2012). The contexts of violence are in proximity to the naming and framing of such violence. The statewide survey presented the results of violence for service providers' and found training and motivations were strong factors for working in the field. The study included suggestions to aid members in learning the nature of their work. Murray and Welch (2010) found that research accounts for the needs and insights of service providersand that service providers need time to do research, which requires time to read and interpret research articles.

Researchers examined perceptions from women who were violence survivors (Simmons et al. 2011). Simmons et al. identified several reasons why woman do not go for help and suggested that family violence programs aimed to reach women in abusive relationships could (a) increase comfort with services; (b) remove barriers to services; (c) implement victim-targeted marketing; and (d) increase community awareness (p. 1). Perrin et al. (2011) suggested women who experience violence tend to also exhibit job-related deficiencies leading to corrective actions or termination. The clusters appeared to reflect stages of behavioral change in an abusive relationship. Physical and sexual abuse against women in partner relationships is a human rights violation (Abeya, Afework, and Yalew 2011). These same authors studied the prevailing patterns associated with violence against women. Seventy-five percent of women have struggled with at least one occurrence of violence. Antai and Awaji (2012) identified and revealed violence as a severe public health crisis for women's physical, psychological, sexual, and reproductive health. The health problems point to the fact that few to no service providers recognized the role of community influences on women's experiences of violence and its effect on terminated pregnancy. Antai and Awaji observed roles throughout community-level norms. Results specified the community's role of influence in the relationship for violence. Two critical areas noted terminated pregnancy and stress create a need to screen women seeking abortions for a history of abuse (Antai and Awaji 2012).

Externalities from troubled youth have been examined (Carrell and Hoekstra 2011). The unique dataset in which children's school records used in correlation with violence cases examined the negative spillovers of children coming from broken homes. Carrell and Hoekstra found children from broken families do considerably worse in reading and math test scores compared to their peers, and the children showed an increase of misbehavior in the classroom and adulthood. The achievement spillovers are significant within family differences and when controlling for school-by-year effects. Wells et al. (2012) found that Montreal has the fifth highest rate of police-reported violence and the second highest rate of self-reported spousal violence. Investment in quality prevention-and-intervention initiatives could be cost effective. Wells et al. (2012) reported that preventive programming in the context of violence showed promising results in reducing incidents of self-reported violence.

During pregnancy, women and infants are more susceptible to the stressor's violence (Aizer 2010). Pregnancy provides a window of opportunity for healthcare providers to find signs of violence and offer an appropriate intervention. Ongoing checkups during the pregnancy further increased identification rates. Some evidence suggested that interventions for pregnant women who had experienced violence reduced the amount of violence experienced by these women. A small number of data limited the effects of the intervention. Further research is required to determine the most effective intervention systems for women who acknowledged violence during pregnancy. Population data presented from seventeen ever-partnered women explored violence associated with unintended pregnancy and abortion in low- and middle-income families (Pallitto et al. 2013). Levendoskya et al. (2011) found relations between violence and income predicted connection patterns. Positive results linked primarily low levels of violence and stayed continuous or became lesser as violence increased over time.

Healey, Humphreys, and Howe (2013) found the responsibility of reporting abuse from violence treatment programs might be contrary to their programmatic philosophy. Violence program participants might not consider themselves mandated reporters. Violence programs and Adult Protective Services tensions have created program interpretation issues and policies of mandated reporting through each of their lenses. Healey, Humphreys, and Howe found reasons why members made recommendations for improving interactions between the two organizations, which would be advantageous to vulnerable adults who experience violence. Zalmanowitz et al. (2013) examined the effect of motivational interviewing (MI) on self-reporting measures. Following an incident of violence, male members were ordered to attend the Responsible Choices for Men group therapy program. The quasi-experimental design showed a relationship between three points: pregroup, the first group session, and the final group session. Global functioning had a binding relationship with the multilevel growth modeling that indicated the stages of development. The researchers concentrated on the possible benefits of MI as an early treatment strategy during the pregroup stage and stressed the importance of understanding an individual's willingness to change. Hazel (2013) documented and theorized possession practices in younger people's intimate relationships and correllated the parallels with violence by using means of authoritative analysis influenced by feminist poststructuralism and critical realism—namely, surveillance and identity ownership.

For future violence survivors, psychological distress and poor coping tactics following the violence attack could deeply affect the survivors' risk (Iverson et al. 2013). Iverson et al. examined the influence of distinct posttraumatic stress disorder (PTSD) symptom clusters (reexperiencing, avoidance, numbing, and hyper arousal), disassociation, and coping strategies (engagement and disengagement coping) on violence victimization among women. When these important forecasters were seen together in a Poisson regression model, only engagement and detachment coping were found to predict physical violence victimization such that detachment coping associated with a higher chance of victimization. Iverson et al. found coping strategies were significant factors in potentially liable forecasters of physical violence victimization. Wu, Button, et al. (2013) assessed and explained citizen preferences of two primary formalized responses to violence law enforcement and social services intervention in a cross-cultural context. Wu, Button, et al. showed respondents have less support for law enforcement responders and indicated social attitude variables involving the male dominance ideology, perceptions of violence causation, and support for the criminalization of violence. The tolerance of violence affects community preferences of responses to violence more than demographic and experiential variables (Wu, Button, et al. 2013).

Women experiencing violence had considerably higher probabilities of unintentional pregnancy in eight of fourteen conditions. Women in twelve of fifteen conditions had risk factors for unintentional pregnancy and abortion throughout a variety of sites. Unintentional pregnancy could lead to dangerous and risky abortion that could result in death or serious health difficulties (Pallitto et al. 2013).

Powers and Simpson (2012) examined the phenomenon of self-protective behaviors to predict the probability and severity of injury inflicted during a violent incident. Powers and Simpson considered an alternate operationalization of self-protective behaviors that divide physical and oral reactions to show behavior relative to the element of force.

Researchers studied women's beliefs about using the healthcare system in violence management. Using the Hurt, Insult, Threaten, and Scream (HITS) instrument, healthcare professionals in six main healthcare centers regularly checked on women to screen for indications of violence (Usta et al. 2012). Most of the seventy-two women screened encouraged participation of the healthcare system on the subject of violence and deliberated to a socially acceptable technique of reporting to disrupt the silence of violence. Approaching violence by means of the healthcare system, when done correctly, could be socially acceptable and inoffensive to women who live in conservative areas.

Substance abuse and a violence incident correlate to one another. Women who have experienced violence have a more likely chance of substance abuse (Macy and Goodbourn 2012). The research concerning violence against victims with substance abuse recommended a number of methods that push for cooperation among violence service agencies and substance abuse treatment programs to make available comprehensive amenities for women with these co-occurring problems. Amenity providers have been creating tactics to build strong relationships between the two service sectors to encourage productive collaborations.

Bapat and Tracey (2012) presented a structured model of dealing with violence that occurs while in the dating stages of a relationship. The design incorporated abuse rates of recurrence and solution attribution to relate to college women's selections of coping tactics. Solution attribution facilitated the relationship between frequency of the abuse and coping. Abuse frequency had a helpful effect on external solution attribution. External solution attribution had a helpful result on actively coping, for example, social backing, denial, and acceptance.

Commonly, victims of violence are women who have disabilities (Ballan and Freyer 2012). The authors studied the prevalence and varieties of violence against women with disabilities and examined the aspects that make this particular population at increased risk for abuse than that of women without disabilities. Highlighted was self-protection against violence for women with diverse disabilities and the use of nonfatal force as self-defense.

Situational information derived from police reports and community factors measured by population characteristics was drawn from the US Census Bureau to assess externally generated workplace violence (Nelson 2012). The data were at the neighborhood level from a number of disadvantaged people, and the immigration concentration had a positive influence on the probability of detention. At a situational level, the time of day, day of the week, the premise type, gender, and racial relations between suspect, complainant, along with offense type and weapons use had a significant effect on whether to arrest a perpetrator of violence. Police officers could choose to employ five different steps when deciding on whether to arrest (Nelson 2012). Each action considerably heightens the chance that the prosecutor will file charges; obtain photographs; search for and arrest the defendant; acquire an emergency protective order; trace extra witnesses; and record additional criminal charges in the police report (Nelson 2012). Women who file an emergency protective order, press charges against the defendant, and show a pattern of abuse increase the likelihood of a criminal conviction upon prosecution. To have a strong case, the top practices model for the investigation of violent events needs to authenticate that the women are victims of post-separation stalking or assault.

Both men and women commit violence with increased amounts of aggression (Shorey et al. 2011). Women's perpetrated aggression was a more often overlooked area in comparison to men's perpetrated aggression (Shorey et al. 2011). Shorey et al. decided to observe the link between trait anger and impulsivity and the commission of physical and psychological violence. Hearn and McKie (2010) identified the presuppositions about gender and violence to surround and advise the methods of policy development and implementation on violence. Hearn and McKie debated how national policies and discourses underscored physical forms of violence, placed the onus on the business of women, and encouraged a narrow conceptualization of violence in relationships. Despite growth in critical research on men, few attempts propose the problems of the gendered nature of violence. Instead, policy and service results mirror methods through which personalized and masculine discourses frame notions, discourses, and policy work. Women experiencing violence constructed as victims and potential survivors of violence are evident in policies.

Organizations attending to the needs of survivors of violence have a mandatory necessity to evaluate their amenities (Riger and Staggs 2011). Three possible assessment strategies include process analysis, outcome evaluation, and performance measurement, which assessed the extent to which companies achieve their stated goals. State-funded agencies in the United States found most states (67 percent) selected only process measurement, while less than 10 percent needed performance measurement. Most (69 percent) state funders indicated satisfaction with their assessment tactic. State funders accentuated the need for involvement of most stakeholders, especially grantees, in developing an evaluation (Riger and Staggs 2011).

The outcomes offered a methodical assessment of proof on the efficiency of violence perpetrator programs (Akoensi et al. 2012). The authors applied treatment to 1,586 violence offenders. Procedural problems relating to the evaluation designs do not negatively influence the findings of the programs, although the assessments exhibited countless positive effects after treatment. The procedural feature of the assessments is inadequate to derive firm deductions and estimate result size. Akoensi et al. could not find that one program method worked better than another method. Evaluation of violence perpetrator treatment improved, and programs should become more personalized to the features of the contributors. Dennis and

Vigod (2013) determined the contribution of interpersonal violence and substance abuse to the likelihood of postpartum depression symptomatology. Community-based samples were taken from 634 women screened for interpersonal violence and substance abuse. Of these women, 78 percent subsequently finished questionnaires at eight weeks postpartum to evaluate for depressive symptomatology. The authors identified that women who experienced previous or present interpersonal violence or personal or partner substance abuse screened for postpartum depression (PPD).

Researchers estimated at least a third of imprisoned male perpetrators have committed violence, but diminutive research can be a on going threat a amid such perpetrators (Hilton et al. 2010). The authors tested 150 imprisoned male violence criminals. The base ratio of postrelease charges for violence was 27 percent. Hilton et al. predicted violence recidivism improved in six months.

Violence treatment platforms are in distress to correctional treatment suppliers because men who fail to have completed treatment are at risk for habitual relapse into the same crime (Jewell and Wormith 2010). A meta-analysis determined the extent to which various demographic, violence-related, and intrapersonal variables foretell attrition from violence treatment platforms for male batterers. The perpetrator's success within the program depended on variables such as employment, education, age, race, addiction, or prior criminal offenses.

Agency directors' viewpoints described how service objectives should be prioritized for violence and sexual assault service subtypes, involving crisis, legal advocacy, medical support, counseling, backing groups, and housing service (Macy, Johns et al. 2011). Violence and sexual assault agency directors ranked service objectives along a continuum from the most important to the least important. Participants considered the emotional backing provision as an important service objective priority throughout most service forms. Social backing and self-care service tactics are the least significant.

Children discourses examined their behaviors or nonpresence of behaviors for the duration of a violence incident (Hester 2011). The experimental information documented group rehabilitation assemblies and single interviews with children who developed mentally and physically after witnessing their fathers' violence against their mothers. The other story showed what the child perceives as possible desires for the future. The prospects of arrest did not deter misdemeanor violence offenders to reduce future offending through intensive investigation and victim support (Exum et al. 2010). Exum et al. evaluated suspects processed through the violence unit and noted significantly lower rates of reoffending across an eighteen- to thirty-month follow-up period.

Wilson and Hoge (2013) found the design of systems response to violence has predominated at the interagency level; further consideration needs must match men's intervention group delivery. Wilson and Hoge decided the program logic of men's violence programs seldom integrated with other programs, leading to lower ranks of program integrity. One technique was to promote program development and efficacy to integrate some of the approaches evident in violence prevention programs. Rigterink, Karowlatz, and Hessler (2010) studied the impression of violence on children's emotion regulation capabilities. The authors observed the relationship between violence exposure and children's regulatory functioning over time, comparing the violence exposure to a child's physiological ability during the primary education period.

Over 196 closed felony violence records from a significant southern city from the years 1999–2006 were reviewed (Friend, Langhinrichsen-Rohling, and Eichold 2011). The purpose of this study was to offer information on the co-occurrence of substance abuse and violence for male and female offenders on the day of a violent event. Friend, Langhinrichsen-Rohling, and Eichold specified that in 141 of the 196 cases in which records and documents indicated drug or alcohol participation, 67.4 percent of the cases found drug or alcohol abuse on the day of the event. Male offenders were more likely to have been using alcohol or drugs on the day of a violent incident than were female offenders. Gender and race analyses exposed that the percentage of female violence offenders (42.9 percent) was considerable, and African Americans, chiefly women, were overrepresented in violence felony charges. The connection between current life proceedings and attitudes toward violence and violent behaviors among offenders were examined (Guoping et al. 2010). Female contributors were assessed for current life proceedings, psychological functioning, social support, and attitudes about violence. Guoping et al. validated that current undesirable life happenings and attitudes were predictable factors for violence after monitoring for demographic variables, psychological functioning, and social supports. Intervention and prevention programs based on psychological functioning and social backing might be valuable to control violence.

Victims' refusals to testify increase the likelihood that cases regarding violence will not go to trial (Gauthier 2010). Gauthier presented a qualitative study examining victims' dismissals of criminal charges in violence cases. The twenty-two judicial and psychosocial professionals interviewed identified many concerns regarding a legal resolution to discharge the charges on victims, perpetrators, justice system professionals, and society. Respondents clearly did not consider the withdrawal of charges as a catastrophe of the criminalization of violence.

Court Cases and Violence

Courts respond inadequately to the problems of violence (Bell et al. 2011). Court orders of protection have the potential to play an important role in the victim's recovery. These orders could connect the victims to new sources of help, inform victims about legal remedies available, and provide validation that no person is to blame nor alone in their struggles (D'Cruz and Noronha 2011). Supporting this notion, scholars of violence found that positive experiences in the justice system, associated with less physical and psychological distress, allow for better posttraumatic adjustment (Golder and Logan, 2010). Bailey (2010) found that the autonomy of victims was not the chief priority of criminal justice policies. Autonomy of victims means that proponents of these policies should concern themselves with the many violence victims who prefer not to engage with the criminal justice system. Other investigators have estimated that as many as 60 percent to 80 percent of violence victims either recant their testimony or refuse to testify against their perpetrator (Bailey 2010). Dennison and Thompson (2011) reported that men and women could be current or former spouses, as well as current or former nonmarital partners. The violence itself falls into four categories: physical, sexual, threats of physical or sexual violence, and psychological/emotional abuse. Violence prevention depends on a common understanding of criminal justice responses.

Perpetrators often commit acts such as assault and possession of a controlled substance in the same incident. The perpetrators find themselves possibly interacting with or encountering the criminal justice system. Criminal justice participation manifested while imprisoned will adversely affect families of the incarcerated (Wu, El-Bassela, et al. 2010); housing (Shinkfield and Graffam 2010); employment (Park 2011); and healthcare and drug treatment (Reeves et al. 2011). Bode (2013) determined that although screening has become routine, 20 percent of women arrived in emergency departments with wounds related to violence, yet reported them as a medical illness. Victims are more likely to use the emergency department than those without a history. Some people would rather discuss violence with emergency department personnel than with a primary-care physician (Cronholm et al. 2011). Cronholm et al. (2011) found that screenings and referrals for violence in the emergency department do not result in increased violence in the three-month postemergency follow-ups, with only one third of these women contacting a community resource.

Transition and Summary

I presented the introductory and background information of the problem of externally generated workplace violence in the coastal region of the US Southwest and described the issues regarding a victim's safety and business liability factors relating to the potential concomitant costs to businesses. The purpose of this qualitative, exploratory, single-case study is to identify strategies to protect companies against liability claims filed by victims of externally generated workplace violence whose predator infiltrates the organization.

Past theorists explored externally generated workplace violence using different methodologies, including qualitative, quantitative, and mixed-methods approaches. Researchers successfully arrived at an agreement on what established the violence and how the phenomenon contributes to business failure (Crowne et al. 2010). I will explore the phenomenon of externally generated workplace violence and identify strategies to increase workplace safety, reduce costs, and prevent liability issues for business owners.

Lorsch (2010) provided a holistic view to describe the basic components of contingency theory. Essential aspects to contingency theory are (a) organizations are open systems in need of management to fulfill and stabilize core needs, (b) management will help employees adapt to environmental conditions, and (c) no best practices exist for organizing information across companies (Lorsch, 2010). Contingency theory could show no single way to organize data to include policies mitigating externally generated workplace violence; different ways of organizing the workforce are not equally effective (Valdiserri and Wilson 2010).

Developing an effective external violence policy requires an organized effort to address the needs of managers in handling cases of externally generated workplace violence in the shipyard industry. This section includes information on the sample and proposed actions to protect the confidentiality of the participants. Concluding this section will be a discussion to explain the (a) research methodologies, (b) data collection, and (c) data analysis to ensure reliability and validity of the study.

Section Two: The Project

The information in Section Two has included the methodological and design details to explore strategies to protect companies against liability claims filed by victims of externally generated workplace violence whose predator infiltrates the organization. Discovering strategies to reduce the potential risk of litigation, which could result from a manager's unfamiliarity about how to protect victims, could be important to sustain the business. A description of the purpose of this exploration, my role as the researcher conducting the study, and identification of strategies to gain volunteers for this research follows. The proposed participants are twelve managers from whom I have elicited perspectives to address the central research question using semistructured interviews, workplace policy documents, and fieldwork observations to form the underpinning of this qualitative, single-case exploration. The central research question was what strategies could prevent externally generated workplace violence from infiltrating the organization.

Purpose Statement

The purpose of this proposed qualitative, single-case study was to identify strategies to safeguard employers against liability claims filed by victims of externally generated workplace violence whose predator infiltrated the business in the coastal region of the US Southwest. Using semistructured interviews, I have interviewed managers who have successfully adopted workplace strategies, policies, and processes to mitigate issues related to externally generated workplace violence in the shipyard and repair industry. Participants have the potential to enhance externally generated workplace violence awareness in the shipyard industry. The results of this study have contributed to social change by (a) increasing managerial awareness and knowledge, (b) increasing safety, (c) reducing costs, and (d) preventing liability issues for the stakeholders.

Role of the Researcher

I explored the perceptions of managers to identify workplace strategies used to safeguard employers against liability claims filed by victims of externally generated workplace violence in the coastal area of the US Southwest. This is my first research study conducted in the field. Yin (2009) stated that data collection would help facilitate an in-depth analysis deriving from semistructured interviews and field observations. I conducted the study in a safe environment and upheld the participant's feelings of trust, thereby protecting the informant's confidentiality.

Participants

The sampling frame consisted of twelve managers experienced in solving problems of externally generated workplace violence. My selection criteria requires each participating manager to have at least five years' experience in a management role. This level of experience will show that managers have enough knowledge to provide a reliable contribution to the proposed study.

Patton (2002) suggested purposeful sampling was the best approach to gain an in-depth understanding of the participants' views, rather than adopting techniques associated with a quantitative analysis, which researchers generalize the finding from a sample to a population. Teddlie and Yu (2007) used purposeful sampling as a nonrandom method of sampling in which the investigators selected information-rich cases for exploration. Chang et al. (2011) used purposeful sampling to study a sample of adults who sought psychological treatment in a mental health facility to understand the occurrence, treatment, and prevention of intimate partner violence. I will use purposeful sampling with eligible managers working in business. This study is a voluntary. No working relationships of authority exist between the potential sample population and me.

The owner of the shipyard organization in the coastal region of the US Southwest gave permission to recruit volunteers working there. I used a solicitation letter to seek the volunteers' involvement (see Appendix A) and to obtain access to company documents. The owner of the organization provided a list of potential participants' e-mail addresses in which to send the invitation. I invited members from the sampling frame by sending a letter of solicitation to managers working in the shipyard and repair industry. The invitation included the objectives of the exploration, the participant's rights under this study, and enough information on which to base his or her decision to participate. I selected the first twelve managers who volunteered for this exploration who meet my selection criteria. The criteria listed in the study of the qualifications as a participant limits the participation pool to twelve volunteers.

At the onset of the interview, I provided and required each participant to sign a consent form (see Appendix A) to acknowledge his or her rights under this investigation. Twelve participants were sufficient to reach data saturation (Francis et al. 2010). Glaser and Strauss (1967) suggested investigators reach data saturation when no new themes materialize during the gathering and assembly process of analyzing data. Francis et al. described the initial minimum interviewed sample size for the conduct of qualitative studies is twelve participants. Rubin and Rubin (2012) concluded that numerous interviews are not required to make objective conclusions when conducting a qualitative study. Two to three interviews per subsample area showed the depth and diversity of participants' perspectives (Rubin and Rubin 2012). Storing printed data and the encrypted electronic media device locked in a secure cabinet when not in use and destroying data after five years at the conclusion of this exploration meets CALUMS University's program requirements. My destruction technique included shredding of paper material and deleting all electronic information from the device.

Research Method and Design

I presented a review of the qualitative research method and case-study design selected for this research. A qualitative method and single-case design created a means to facilitate strategies aimed to safeguard employers against liability claims filed by victims (Denzin and Lincoln 2011; Yin 2009). Participants described their perceptions and experiences using semistructured interview questions, which provided the participant the opportunity to expand on his or her experience (Bernard 2013).

Method

Researchers choose from three methods of inquiry: quantitative, qualitative, or mixed methods. The use of a quantitative method relies on deductive logic, normally associated with scientific or survey-based research in the practical analysis to refute or verify a hypothesis (Oaksforda and Chatera 2009). Researchers generalize the findings about the nature of phenomena to validate the findings (Oaksforda and Chatera 2009). A quantitative design was not appropriate in this research because the objective is not to test or verify a theory or null hypotheses (Bernard 2013).

Qualitative methods focus on the process, the product, and the result that emerges (Denzin and Lincoln 2011). The traditional approach of data collection in qualitative research is shifting to an undetermined information collection process. Qualitative researchers focus primarily on four areas: (a) language as a means to explore processes of communication, (b) patterns of interaction within particular social groups, (c) description and interpretation of subjective meanings attributed to situations, and (d) theory building by discovering patterns and connections in qualitative data (Oaksforda and Chatera 2009). A quality approach developed at the outset is not finalized (Marshall and Rossman 2011). I chose a qualitative method of exploration to show strategies aimed to prevent externally generated workplace violence from infiltrating the organization. Yin (2009) suggested that a qualitative approach allows researchers to provide a reliable means to perform substantiated-based research. Procedures used in a mixed-method approach align both quantitative and qualitative styles, which in this study is not practical to answer the research question nor appropriate because of time and cost constraints.

Research Design

The use of narrative, phenomenological, grounded, or ethnography designs are not appropriate for this research to gather data. A narrative study approach details the life experience of a single individual over a long period, and a phenomenological study details the meaning that a lived experience holds for an individual (Moustakas, 1994). A grounded theory design illustrates a theory, and an ethnography study shows the behavior of a culture-sharing group (Denzin and Lincoln 2011).

The case study research design explores strategies of inquiry on why and how a phenomenon occurred (Ashley 2012). Sedighi and Loosemore (2012) used a qualitative study to understand how to construct strategies to attract and retain employees working in the building trade industry. Yin (2009) suggested the strength of a case study design is achieved when researchers collect data in a natural setting. A case study, in contrast to other research designs, is best when investigators require the ability to facilitate exploring a holistic understanding of the phenomenon under study. I proposed to use an exploratory single-case design structure, which allowed me the versatility to obtain an in-depth picture to analyze the principal research question employed in this study.

The use of semistructured interview questions illustrated workplace strategies that could help protect organizations against liability claims filed by victims of externally generated workplace violence whose predator infiltrates business (Denzin and Lincoln 2011; Shuck 2011). I intend to reach data saturation following the direction of Francis et al. (2010) which will involve eight initial interviews, with a stopping criterion of two interviews devoid of new concepts rising (Moola, Fusco, and Kirsh 2011).

Participants who volunteer for this study must sign an informed consent form to understand and protect their rights under this research (see Appendix A). Electronic information stored on an encrypted flash drive adds another layer of protection of confidentiality. I placed data in my home's fireproof safe when not in use. The safe also stored electronic and printed material at the conclusion of this research for the next five years until such time destruction of the data occurs, which is in accordance with the program requirements of CALUMS University. My destruction technique included shredding paper material using a paper shredder and deleting electronic information from the encrypted device.

Population and Sampling

The population under exploration is large for companies in the United States. The optimal sample size is needed for researchers to sufficiently explore the research question (Marshall and Rossman (2011). Glaser and Strauss (1967) suggested investigators reach data saturation when no new themes materialize during the gathering and assembly process of analyzing data.

Population

The sample population for this study is approximately thirty managers who have five years of experience supervising employee in the shipyard and repair industry. The proposed purposeful sample size for this study is twelve shipyard managers who work in the coastal area of the US Southwest and have supervised employees inflicted with externally generated workplace violence. Policy documentation, semistructured interviews, and fieldwork observations allowed me to demonstrate data triangulation. I will not be observing the participants in their regular work settings but instead will take notes during the interview process to examine nonverbal messaging and body language from the participants. My plan is to interview participants off-site at a mutually agreed upon location.

Sampling

Patton (2002) suggested purposeful sampling was the best approach to gain an in-depth understanding of the participants' views, rather than adopting techniques associated with a quantitative analysis. Teddlie and Yu (2007) used purposeful sampling as a nonrandom method of sampling in which the investigators selected information-rich cases for exploration. Chang et al. (2011) used purposeful sampling to study a sample of adults who sought psychological treatment in a mental health facility to understand the occurrence, treatment, and prevention of intimate partner violence. I used a purposeful sampling with eligible managers working in business.

I asked qualifying questions to determine the participant's candidacy for my research. Data showed the length of time the potential participant supervised employees and worked in the shipyard and repair industry. Other details illustrated the participant's exposure to managing employees who were the victim of abuse resulting from an environment, which infiltrated the workplace.

Francis et al. (2010) discussed the initial minimum interviewed sample size for the conduct of qualitative studies is twelve participants, which are sufficient to identify themes for saturation and sufficiency purposes. Rubin and Rubin (2012) concluded that numerous interviews are not required to make objective conclusions when conducting a qualitative study. Researchers used two to three interviews per subsample area to determine the depth and diversity of perspectives (Rubin and Rubin 2012). The criteria listed in the study of the qualifications as a member participant limits the participation pool to twelve. Following Francis et al. (2012), open coding involved eight initial interviews, with a stopping criterion of two interviews devoid of new concepts rising to ensure data saturation.

Gaining enough participants to ensure data saturation using the purposeful sampling method poses some threats. The participants are managers from the industry. These managers experienced personnel shortages because employees miss work because of violence. The personnel shortages could stem from employees arriving late to work, being absent, or needing to leave work early. The shipyard and repair industry would have limited female managers. I will anticipate collecting a variety of perspectives from managers with externally generated workplace violence experience in business and will consider the possibility of gender bias. I will not offer any gratuity for participation in this research because offering a gratuity could skew the results.

Ethical Research

Conforming to IRB process ensured the study complies with moral ethics concerning human participants in research (Bozeman, Slade, and Hirsch 2009). Participants electing to withdraw from the study could do so without penalty. Participants would be able to refuse to answer any question and to take a break at any time during the interview. The consent form included a withdrawal notice so participants could provide notice of intent to withdraw from the study.

I will assure contributors that information will remain confidential and will protect their identity by assigning an identification number known only to me. The coding format featured Participant 1, 2, 3 formats. The process to protect the participant's confidentiality appeared in the informed consent form. Participants who volunteer for this study must sign an informed consent form to understand and protect their rights under this research (see Appendix A). Electronic information stored on an encrypted flash drive will add another layer of protection of confidentiality. I placed the data in my home's fireproof safe when not in use. The safe will also store electronic and printed material at the conclusion of this research for the next five years until such time destruction of the data occurs, which is in accordance with the program requirements of CALUMS University. My destruction technique will include shredding paper material using a paper shredder and deleting electronic information from the encrypted device.

Data Collection

Researcher-collected data is gathered from study participants. An interview guide allows researchers to plan the groundwork to ensure data collection remains consistent. I identified the instrument, interview strategy, and the process necessary to resolve explanations as follows.

Instruments

I am the main instrument collecting data in this research. Qualitative researchers serve as the instruments collecting data from document reviews, observations, and participant interviews (Marshall and Rossman 2011). The data recording technique is the use of an encrypted tape recording device (Bernard 2013). The tool allows interviews to commence in unplanned circumstances. The use of open-ended questions allows investigators to refer to important points and follow up on participant responses. Themes and categories emerged through the coding process of the responses.

The proposed data collection format for this study is conducting semistructured interviews with managers in the workplace. Participant responses could affect follow-up questions posed by me. Semistructured interviews provide an interactive, emergent data collection opportunity to allow an evolving exploration to uncover a participant's feelings (Ashley 2012). The answers elicited the necessary information to assist me in addressing the primary research question for this study (Rubin and Rubin 2012; Shuck 2011). Member checking and triangulation assisted me to assure the validity of my study's findings.

I designed and adhered to a specific protocol for the conduct of the qualitative case study. A case study protocol served to ensure the dependability of the study by outlining the procedures and rules followed during the conduct of research and by ensuring that study data collection, analysis, and reporting efforts remain focused on the study line of inquiry (Marshall and Rossman 2011; Yin 2009). I prepared and followed a case study protocol that included (a) an overview of the intended project, (b) a description of the protocol purpose and intended use, (c) a description of study data collection procedures, (d) an outline of the case study report content, (e) a list of the case study interview questions, (f) a summary of the data analysis techniques and tools used, and (g) a description of the study dependability, credibility, and transferability methods (see Appendix B).

I incorporated member checking and transcript review techniques to ensure dependability and credibility of the research. Member checking is when researchers return to the participants to understand if codes and meaning from the codes are recognizable (Ashley 2012; Marshall and Rossman 2011). I confirmed with the participants whether I had transcribed the interview responses accurately. Participants had an opportunity to modify their transcript or ask additional questions (Denzin and Lincoln 2011). Members stated if the transcribed data is recognizable. Lincoln and Guba (1994) referred to credibility as techniques, which show the accuracy in identifying and describing data.

Data Collection Technique

Marshall and Rossman (2011) recommended that multiple sources of data are necessary for demonstrating a case study is credible. Ashley (2012) concluded the advantage of collecting multiple forms of data would substantiate study findings. The disadvantage of using a triangulation technique is the time required to gather data and complete a research project. Data triangulation procedures included a review of the workplace policy documents, semistructured interviews, and field note observations (Yin 2009).

I collected data using an encrypted recording device from participants working in the shipyard and repair industry. Data also included the review of audiotaped interviews from twelve managers who supervise employees dealing with violence issues. Participants signed a consent form and agreed to have their interviews audiotaped (Bernard 2013). Semistructured interview questions provide the participant the opportunity to expand on his or her experience (Ashley 2012). Data saturation follows the direction of Francis et al. (2010) which will involve eight initial interviews, with a stopping criterion of two interviews devoid of new concepts rising. A pilot study is not appropriate for this research because the proposed conduct does not include a quantitative or mixed-method approach of inquiry (Yin 2009). Pilot studies generate data for reliability and validity purposes (Patton 2002).

I incorporated member checking and transcript review techniques to ensure dependability and credibility of the research. Member checking is when researchers return to the participants to understand if codes and meaning from the codes are recognizable (Ashley 2012; Marshall and Rossman 2011). I confirmed with the participants whether I had transcribed the interview responses accurately. Participants had an opportunity to modify their transcript (Denzin and Lincoln 2011). Members stated if the transcribed data is recognizable. Lincoln and Guba (1994) referred to credibility as techniques, which show the accuracy in identifying and describing data.

Data Organization Techniques

My coding process includes developing codes for organizing participants' responses into categories and themes using ATLAS.ti software. I aligned the data to the larger conceptual perspective in the research. Data stored on an encrypted flash drive will provide protection should the device be lost or stolen. The use of an Excel information storage system helped me organize and manage data throughout the conduct of the research (Marshall and Rossman 2011). Storing printed data in a secure cabinet when not in use and destroying all data after five years at the conclusion of this exploration meets CALUMS University's program requirements. My destruction technique included shredding of paper material and deleting all electronic information from the device.

Data Analysis Technique

Semistructured interview questions could help me explore how strategies could prevent externally generated workplace violence from infiltrating the organization. The interview questions allowed study participants to provide their opinions. The following subquestions and interview questions could help guide the conduct of this study:

Research Subquestions

1. What protocols and policies are implemented for the prevention, intervention, and dealing with the aftermath of a violent incident?
2. What training are managers and employees given about externally generated workplace violence?
3. What could create an environment in which victims of externally generated workplace violence feel supported and will report the potential danger of violence spilling into the workplace?
4. How could managers create an environment in which perpetrators know that violence is not acceptable behavior (on or off the job), and how could community resources offer help in changing behavior?

Interview Questions.
1. How long have you been working as a manager in business?
2. How did you construct your policy to manage the issue of externally generated workplace violence?
3. How effective is the current policy and training on externally generated workplace violence?
4. How could regulations or laws help to manage externally generated workplace violence in business?
5. How could multidisciplinary teams (MT) perform in dealing with externally generated workplace violence?
6. What roles do each member of the MT play in dealing with externally generated workplace violence issues?
7. What training do supervisors and employees receive about how to respond to suspected externally generated workplace violence?
8. What symptoms are associated with externally generated workplace violence prior to an incident occurring?
9. What intervention and prevention measures are implemented for you as a manager?
10. What procedures and processes are implemented that demonstrate a climate of zero tolerance?
11. What other aspects can you offer to discuss about your company's current policies to prevent and address externally generated workplace violence?

I used data from the answers provided to expedite thematic coding and classification of collected information using ATLAS.ti software, which is a computer-assisted qualitative data analysis application. The purpose of the ATLAS.ti software is to facilitate a researcher's ability to analyze sizeable and complex data. The software enables the user to search for themes and patterns to derive meaning.

I identified and developed relevant categories and themes to identify workplace strategies to safeguard employers against liability claims from incidents of externally generated workplace violence in the coastal region of the US Southwest. Results from the interview questions describe future contingency leadership policies that affect the incidence of externally generated workplace violence.

I developed interview questions that encouraged study participants to share insights and perspectives regarding the various factors that limit efforts to detect and mitigate externally generated workplace violence. A review of documents illustrated how individual, institutional, and societal factors affect externally generated workplace violence; this research will align the collection and analysis of study data with the conceptual framework for this study.

Judge, Hiscock, and Bauld (2010) provided a framework for researchers to undertake holistic, multilevel investigations of complex social phenomena. The contingency theory approach is the guiding conceptual framework. I conducted semistructured interviews, fieldwork observations, and a review of workplace policy documents to characterize the various factors that influence and impede efforts to detect and control externally generated workplace violence from infiltrating the organization.

I employed coding as the primary data analysis technique for the qualitative case study. Qualitative researchers use coding as a mechanism for categorizing and describing their study's data. Coding methods include deductive coding and inductive (open) coding. As described by Bernard (2013), researchers employing deductive coding use the theoretical or conceptual framework for their studies as the basis for derivation of codes. During the application of open coding, researchers immerse themselves in the data during the review process and focus on capturing emerging themes (Bernard 2013) that could transcend the conceptual framework.

To facilitate the identification of themes related to this study's research question and conceptual framework, the categorization of the research subquestions and conceptual framework will guide the findings. I used software to support the handling, sorting, and analysis of document and interview data from the study to perform frequency and co-occurrence metrics. Application of ATLAS.ti allowed me to confirm the exploration, and my analysis of study data will be suitably robust via data analysis and triangulation techniques (Leech and Onegbuzie 2007).

Reliability and Validity

The concepts of reliability and dependability and validity and credibility are notably the same models and are important considerations during the study design phase. Qualitative researchers demonstrate the trustworthiness of their research through a focus on dependability rather than reliability. Uses of multiple data sources such as document reviews, observations, and participant interviews ensure the findings are credible, allow the corroboration of findings of the same phenomenon, and support study validity (Denzin and Lincoln 2011; Marshall and Rossman 2011).

Reliability

Qualitative researchers include mechanisms in the design of their studies to ensure the dependability and credibility of study data and findings (Marshall and Rossman 2011). I incorporated member checking and transcript review techniques to ensure dependability and credibility of the research. Member checking is where researchers return to the participants to ensure that codes and meaning from the codes are recognizable (Ashley 2012; Marshall and Rossman 2011). Participants confirmed the accuracy of the transcribed interviews. Participants had an opportunity to modify their transcript or ask additional questions (Denzin and Lincoln 2011). Members stated if the transcribed data is recognizable. Lincoln and Guba (1994) referred to credibility as techniques that show the accuracy of identifying and describing data.

I used reliability assurance methods in the study format by maintaining detailed interview notes on the participants and employed generally accepted tape-recording methods by using cellular technology to enhance this capability. The cellular technology is digital, making the instrument an excellent device for such recordings. The device could stop and start during transcription. Researchers could use case study protocols and case study databases to demonstrate case study dependability (Yin 2009).

A case study protocol included an outline of the research procedures followed to gain conformability. The protocol will show the case study data collection, analysis, and reporting activities to remain focused on the study's line of inquiry (Ashley 2012). Ashley emphasized the importance of using a case study protocol to keep the research subject focused on the topic under discussion. Researchers use study databases to document notes, materials, data, and narratives collected during the conduct of case studies (Yin 2009). Case study databases serve as a means for other investigators to review case study evidence directly rather than rely solely on a review of final case study reports prepared by the original case study researchers (Yin 2009). Gibbert and Ruigrok (2010) examined the strategies of researchers to demonstrate case study rigor and noted the importance of the use of case study databases to assert a case study's dependability through the documentation of (a) collected data, (b) analysis products, (c) narratives, and (d) conclusions.

Validity

Study validity is a central measure in quantitative social science research to ensure accuracy of the findings (Bernard 2012). Qualitative researchers ensure credibility and trustworthiness of the data by using multiple data sources that support the findings (Denzin and Lincoln 2011). Ashley (2012) posited that investigators require multiple sources of data to ensure credibility and trustworthiness. The comparison of information in the literature on externally generated workplace violence could show a deep understanding of how different investigators view the problem of externally generated workplace violence. If the findings from different scholars arrive at the same conclusion, the credibility of the proposed study could increase (Stake 2010).

Data triangulation provided further assurance of the findings' validity. Interviews, documents, and prolonged engagement with participants are the methods of choice to substantiate the findings. Patton (2002) cautioned that a common misconception of data triangulation is to assume that researchers could arrive at consistency across data sources. Triangulation inconsistencies could lend to the relative strengths of different approaches, such that inconsistencies would uncover the opportunity to note the deeper meaning in the data (Patton 2002). Triangulation should help identify and address any biases. I applied a case study protocol and used multiple data sources during the collection process to establish trustworthiness of the finding (Denzin and Lincoln 2011).

Transition and Summary

The objective of Section Two was to detail the (a) intent, (b) research design, (c) population sample, and (d) analytical methods used for the proposed study. I propose a qualitative, single case study to facilitate exploration of how workplace strategies could safeguard employers against liability claims filed from incidents of externally generated workplace violence. I collected information from (a) policy documentation, (b) semistructured interviews, and (c) fieldwork observations. Section Three included the results of the data analysis, application to the business practice, overview of the study, and a presentation of the findings. Information also includes implications for social change and recommendation for further research.

Section Three: Application to Professional Practice and Implications for Change

A detailed description of the results from conducting this study is listed in this section. It includes an overview of the study, presentation of the findings, application to professional practice, implications for social change, and recommendation for action. The section ends with recommendations for further studies, reflection on my experience, and study conclusions.

Overview of Study

I conducted a qualitative, descriptive case study of what strategies, procedures, and processes managers are employing to prevent and address externally generated workplace violence incidents, some of which may result in fewer workplace liability claims. In order to promote the rich exploration of managers, I identified and examined the following research subquestions:

1. What protocols and policies are implemented for the prevention, intervention, and dealing with the aftermath of a violent incident?
2. What training is implemented to educate managers and employees about externally generated workplace violence?

3. How can an environment be created in which victims of externally generated workplace violence feel supported and will report potential violence in the workplace?
4. How can managers create an environment in which perpetrators know that violence is not acceptable behavior (on or off the job) and that there are community resources that offer help in changing their behavior?

I collected study data from the review of publicly available documents and the information received from eleven semistructured interviews with leaders in business. I used purposeful and snowball sampling to identify and recruit study participants. I identified managers and sent initial e-mails requesting study of twelve interviewees who participated in face-to-face interviews at locations of their choosing.

I conducted the interviews in the Southwestern United States and gathered the documents included in the case study during the same period. During the interviews, the twelve participants responded to each of the eleven interview questions included in the case study protocol. Each participant received an informed consent form (Appendix A) for review and signature prior to the start of the interview. I recorded each interview after getting permission from each participant to do so and created transcriptions of recorded interviews. Participants reviewed and provided corrections to their transcripts prior to my starting the data analysis process.

I used the software tool ATLAS.ti to perform deductive and open coding of collected data and to conduct frequency analysis of coded data segments. Code frequency results supported the identification of key themes. The conduct of member checking enhanced the credibility of my qualitative case study.

Coding of the collected data revealed several perceptions regarding impediments to the detection. The following

primary themes emerged from my analysis of the data contained in Appendix C:
1. Externally generated workplace violence awareness
2. Externally generated workplace violence procedures
3. Externally generated workplace violence safety and security
4. Externally generated workplace violence prevention
5. Externally generated workplace violence policy

Presentation of the Findings

To facilitate examination of the primary study research question and subquestions, I created and categorized codes by research subquestion and conceptual framework. I used the software tool ATLAS.ti to code all interview transcripts and case study documents and to conduct code frequency for identifying key themes. Five themes emerged from the analysis of the study research subquestions and interview questions.

Research Subquestion One

The research topic explored with this subquestion was as follows: What protocols and policies are in place for the prevention, intervention, and dealing with the aftermath of a violent incident?

A number of laws affect violence in business. The law that was mention most from the interviews conducted was assault laws. All participants listed this as a concern. The participant prevalent thought was the number of threats that were imposed on management for just being in the industry. OSHA laws were mentioned by eight of twelve respondents. Most respondents stated the idea of safety in the workplace is major concern for managers. A security plan must be enacted to lessen the fear of retribution. The Family Leave Act was mentioned by two of twelve respondents. The few respondents who mentioned the act thought that the measure should be used to protect employees from fear of retribution by their potential assaulter. As mentioned in the literature review, perpetrators often use the victim's place of work to locate a victim once they decide to leave their perpetrator. Two respondents mentioned worker's compensation pay for injuries acquired on the job. Finally, one respondent mentioned the Americans with Disabilities Act. Member employees may file discrimination lawsuits if employers fail to protect employees under the premise of mental and physical abuse.

The participants indicated employees are responsible for their own behavior and interactions with fellow employees and their supervisors. Employees should promptly report any incident, anonymously if necessary. Any acts of violence, threats, and similar disruptive behavior in the workplace should be reported to security. Participants also noted that cooperating fully in investigations and assessments of allegations of externally generated workplace violence is a requirement. Informing security, front desk personnel, supervisors, and others as needed in the business about restraining orders and other protective court orders related to situations allows assistance to be offered at the worksite.

Managers are additionally responsible for ensuring that all of their employees are fully informed of and understand externally generated workplace violence policy and procedures. Participants noted that being cognizant of situations that have the potential to produce violence and promptly addressing them with all concerned parties is a needed concern. Participants noted that being sensitive to stress generated by the workplace and considering changes that could alleviate work-related stress is important in business. Participants noted that documenting and responding to allegations of externally generated workplace violence in a timely fashion is critical, and evaluating the results and taking necessary action is paramount.

Some strategies for creating a supportive environment and prevention may include offering a confidential means for seeking resource and referral information. Additional security at the workplace provides a level of comfort to those who fear retribution. Flexible work schedules and workplace relocation measures prevent perpetrators from locating the victims. Close communication between security and training on violence for managers, employees, and occupational health staff prevent violence.

Security services provide consultation and reasonable assistance to employees experiencing violence to help relax the environment. Employees should respond and intervene, as needed, to calls concerning safety in the workplace. Employees should accept transferred harassing telephone calls from the perpetrator, and document the calls to help relax the environment. Employees should work closely with appropriate law enforcement agencies to ensure workplace safety. The security department can be a liaison for police activity and coordinate direct activities with regard to protection orders and incident response. The legal department can provide assistance regarding protection orders and can be a police liaison. The human resources department can coordinate training efforts and ensure policy is written to address specific violence issues.

Research Subquestion Two

What training is implemented to educate managers and employees about externally generated workplace violence?

Participants noted that most were not aware of any training on externally generated workplace violence. The company did possess a policy. Most (64 percent) agreed the training should be included in orientations and repeated on an annual basis, much the same as sexual harassment. E-mail should be use as a primary means to communicate business facts about violence.

Posters and presentations are used to get the message out along with electronic bulletin boards and television monitors.

Research Subquestion Three

What can create an environment in which victims of externally generated workplace violence feel supported and will report potential violence in the workplace?

When policies on externally generated workplace violence are defined, reported, trained, and implemented with designated roles and responsibilities, victims often feel comfortable reporting incidents of violence. Employees should report incidents of violence to their supervisors, as well as any employees who display any of the listed signs of potential violence. The department can try to get the employee the help he or she needs to avoid harming anyone at work or elsewhere. Chronic absenteeism, excessive tardiness, inappropriate/excessive clothing, obsessions with time, repeated physical injuries, chronic health problems (e.g. chronic pain), isolation, emotional distress, depression, distraction, and excessive numbers of personal phone calls are all signs of an agitated state (U.S. Department of Health and Human Services 2014).

Research Subquestion Four

How can managers create an environment in which perpetrators know that violence is not acceptable behavior (on or off the job) and that there are community resources that offer help in changing their behavior?

First, report any incident, train employees, and have a policy in place to deal with and recognize the issue of violence. Companies should have adequate security and protection. All respondents mentioned the need for confidentiality to allow other employees undisclosed involvement with a potential incident. A reporting procedure should be implemented for those who want to be involved and for those who would like to be able to report anonymously. A hotline is recommended for those who do not want to be identified. The protocol for reporting should be an immediate supervisor, human resources department, ethics department, and legal department.

Applications to Professional Practice

The application to professional practice with regard to externally generated workplace violence must start with a definition. The idea that externally generated workplace violence is not, will it affect the workplace, but how and when it will affect the workplace. There must be different methods of reporting. Reporting anonymously must be one of the methods. Management must have open door policies to encourage the reporting of incidents affecting the productivity of the workplace. All key players such as HR, management, employees, and security are trained annually. The policy should be implemented with designated roles and responsibilities outlined.

Implications for Social Change

Leaders must consider the costs of violence in the workplace, which include the affliction of human suffering. Victims of externally generated workplace violence suffer from both emotional and physical damage, which could affect their employment and personal life. Expenses plaguing the industry could force organizational leaders to adopt workforce violence policies, which address violent invasions, by creating responses designed to mitigate the financial costs associated with the problem. The leaders of business could establish social change by adopting internal strategies that address policies and procedures regarding externally generated workplace violence, and safeguards to increase the leader's situational awareness, which is a concern for employees and the community. The results of this study contribute to social change by increasing managerial awareness of externally generated workplace violence, thereby increasing workplace safety, reducing costs, and preventing liability issues for business owners (Lim and Tai 2014).

Recommendations for Action

Organizations such as the American Bar Association (2014) recommend addressing the specific problem of externally generated workplace violence by having a company policy. The idea of a specific policy may lessen the chance of litigation by the victims of externally generated workplace violence and put into place a response for the prevention of an incident. In business, a good policy would increase workplace safety, reduce costs, and prevent liability issues for business owners (Lim and Tai 2014).

Recommendations for Further Study

The subject of externally generated workplace violence has not traditionally been approached by researchers. Delving into the topic, researchers should investigate more industry-related externally generated workplace violence. A comparison of industries such as police versus firefighters would be an excellent topic to explore. The idea of the men who protect and serve and how often they are the subject of violence could be studied. The military is another area to explore with regard to externally generated workplace violence.

Reflections

I have conducted this research with great ethical prowess. I have maintained the context of my proposal by adhering to the direction stated in the document. I have attempted, to the best of my ability, to stay as neutral as possible about my biases. However, the men

I have interviewed have held some of the highest positions in the US military. These positions range from chief engineer to captain of ships. Their conservative thought process motivates them. What has transpired while conducting this research is an example of an excellent balanced approach to the exploration of the research questions posed in this study. They adhere to the concept of intervention, but not so much as one is to believe the government can solve the problem of externally generated workplace violence. Nevertheless, the men believe high morale in their teammates yields better results.

Summary and Study Conclusions

Companies' efforts to reduce chances of having litigation brought against them have improved. Still it is estimated that 33 percent of companies do not have policies implemented to combat externally generated workplace violence. This study has collected data to support practical facts that will help a company lessen the chance of having effective litigation brought against it. The policy failure rates have continued to increase, despite recommendations from prior studies on how to be effective advocates against externally generated workplace violence. The following primary themes emerged from my analysis of the data contained in Appendix C:

1. Externally generated workplace violence awareness
2. Externally generated workplace violence procedures
3. Externally generated workplace violence safety and security
4. Externally generated workplace violence prevention
5. Externally generated workplace violence policy definition

Borrowing from the open system theory, the study discusses tools for changing thinking and explanations of general patterns and obstacles (Bertanlanffy 1956). When business managers proceed with rigid ideas on how change should occur, most find that the dynamic, ever-changing circumstances of dealing with externally generated workplace violence are not sufficient. The feedback from a dynamic situation makes decision making at the manager level more precise to the given circumstance. For instance, a company may benefit from open systems theory by meeting business cultural changes and needs, allowing a company to assist employees and meet their specific needs. A level of social awareness indicates that companies will want to do business with a company that observes certain safety or environmental protocols (Bertanlanffy 1956).

In conclusion, what strategies could prevent externally generated workplace violence from infiltrating the organization? I suggest that externally generated workplace violence efforts in the US Southwest start with policies to reduce litigation, ensuring the policies address the major themes of awareness, procedures, safety, security, and definition. All companies have a duty to protect their employees; without a policy that addresses the issues of externally generated workplace violence, a company might be vulnerable to expensive litigation. Externally generated workplace violence is not a might, but a when: when will it affect the workplace? Therefore, any incident should be reported, and there must be different methods of reporting. For example, a female attends work with a bruised eye, and a supervisor notices and asks, "What is wrong?" She replies, "Nothing." The supervisor does not respond any further, and the employee's significant other seriously hurts the woman that afternoon. Under the duty to protect, did the supervisor conduct himself in a manner that releases all liability to the employer? The key is to have a policy to deal with just such a situation. Management must have open door policies to encourage the reporting of incidents affecting the productivity of the workplace.

References

Abeys, S., M. Afework, and A. Yalew. 2011. "Intimate Partner Violence Against Women in Western Ethiopia: Prevalence, Patterns, and Associated Factors." *BMC Public Health* 11: 913–27, doi:10.1186/1471-2458-11-913.

Abraham, M. 2010. "Restorative Justice and Violence Against Women." *Contemporary Sociology: A Journal of Reviews* 39: 635–736, doi:10.1177/0094306110386886.

Aizer, A. 2010. "The Gender Wage Gap and Domestic Violence." *The American Economic Review* 100: 1847–59, doi:10.1257/aer.100.4.1847.

Alaniz, R. 2010. "When Violence Affects the Workplace, What Liabilities Do Employers Face?" AccountingWEB: http://www.accountingweb.com.

Al-Modallal, H., A. K. Sowan, S. Hamaideh, A. R. Peden, H. Al-Omari, and A. B. Al-Rawashdeh. 2012. "Psychological Outcomes of Intimate Partner Violence Experienced by Jordanian Working Women." *Health Care for Women International* 33: 217–27.

Al-Omari, M. A., H. Johari, and L. S. Choo. 2012. "Workplace Violence: A Case in Malaysian Higher Education Institute." *Business Strategy Series* 13: 274–83.

Akoensi, T., J. Koehler, F. Lösel, and D. Humphreys. 2012. "Domestic Violence Perpetrator Programs in Europe, Part II: A Systematic Review of the State of Evidence." *International Journal Offender and Comparative of Criminology* 57: 1206–25. doi:10.1177/0306624X12468110.

American Bar Association. 2014. *Employment Law and Domestic Violence: A Practitioner's Guide.* http://www.americanbar.org.

American Institute on Domestic Violence. 2014. www.aidv-usa.com.

Antai, D. and S. Awaji. 2012." Community-Level Influences on Women's Experience of Intimate Partner Violence and Terminated Pregnancy in Nigeria: A Multilevel." *BMC Pregnancy and Childbirth,* online publication, 12: 128–40. doi:10.1186/1471-2393-12-128.

Ashley, L. D. 2012. "The Use of Saturation Theory to Conceptualize Alternative Practice in Education: The Case of Private School Outreach in India." *British Journal of Sociology of Education* 31: 337–51. doi:10.1080/01425691003700599.

Aupperle, R., C. Allard, E. Grimes, A. Simmons, T. Flagan, M. Behrooznia, S. Cissell, M. Stein. 2012. "Dorsolateral Prefrontal Cortex Activation During Emotional Anticipation and Neuropsychological Performance in Posttraumatic Stress Disorder." *Archives of General Psychiatry* 69: 360–71. doi:10.1001/archgenpsychiatry.2011.1539.

Babbie, E. R. 2010. *The Practice of Social Research.* Belmont, CA: Wadsworth Cengage.

Bailey, K. 2010. "Lost in Translation: Domestic Violence the Personal Is Political." *The Journal of Criminal Law* 37: 17–23. doi:0091-4169/10/10004-1255.

Ballan, M., and M. Freyer. 2012. "Self-Defense Among Women with Disabilities: An Unexplored Domain in Domestic Violence Cases." *Violence Against Women* 18: 1083–107. doi:10.1177/1077801212461430.

Banyard, V. L., R. P. Eckstein, and M. M. Moynihan. 2010. "Sexual Violence Prevention: The Role of Stages of Change." *Journal of Interpersonal Violence* 25: 1–135. doi:10.1177/0886260508329123

Bapat, M., and T. Tracey. 2012. "Coping with Dating Violence as a Function of Violence Frequency and Solution Attribution: A Structural Modeling Approach." *Violence and Victims* 27: 329–43. doi:10.1891/0886-6708.27.3.329.

Bell, M. E., S. Perez, L. A. Goodman, and M. Dutton. 2011. "Battered Women's Perceptions of Civil and Criminal Court Helpfulness: The Role of Court Outcome and Process." *Violence Against Women* 17: 71–88. doi:10.1177/1077801210393924.

Bernard, H. R. 2013. *Social Research Methods: Qualitative and Quantitative Approaches.* 2nd ed. Thousand Oaks, CA: Sage.

Bode, H. 2013. "Improving Health Care and Exam Outcomes for Sexual Violence Survivors: A Webinar for Medical Professionals." PhD diss. Retrieved from University of St. Thomas Research Online (Paper 29).

Bonham, E., and A. Vetere. 2012. "Qualitative Study Using a Systemic Perspective: Exploring the Remediation of Abusive Interactions in Intimate Heterosexual Couples." *Journal Interpersonal Violence.* Advanced online publication. doi:10.1177/0886260511423253.

Bozeman, B., C. Slade, P. and Hirsch. 2009. "Ethics in Research and Practice." *American Journal of Public Health* 99: 1549–56. doi:10.2105/AJPH.2008.152389.

Broeder, J., and A. Donze. 2010. "The Role of Qualitative Research in Evidence-Based Practice." *Journal Neonatal Network: The Journal of Neonatal Nursing Issue* 29: 69–77. doi:10.1891/0730-0832.29.3.197.

Brown, J. 2012. "Male Perpetrators, the Gender Symmetry Debate and the Rejection-Abuse Cycle: Implications for Treatment." *American Journal of Men's Health* 6: 331–43. doi:10.1177/1557988312439404.

Campbell, M., J. Neil, P. Jaffe, and T. Kelly. 2010. "Engaging Abusive Men in Seeking Community Intervention." *A Critical*

Research and Practice Priority Family Violence 2: 86–121. doi:10.1007/s10896-010-9302-.

Carlson, R., and J. Dayle 2010. "Continuum of Conflict and Control: A Conceptualization of Intimate Partner Violence Typologies." The Family Journal 18:248–54. doi:10.1177/1066480710371795.

Carmody, M. 2013. "Young Men, Sexual Ethics and Sexual Negotiation." Sociological Research Online 18(2): 22. doi:10.5151/sro.2932.

Carrell, S. and M. Hoekstra. 2011. "Externalities in the Classroom: How Children Exposed to Domestic Violence Affect Everyone's Kids." American Economic Journal Applied Economics 2: 211–28. doi:10.1257/app.2.1.21jobs@stpaulseniors.org.

Casey, E., and T. Smith. 2010. "How Can I Not? Men's Pathways to Involvement in Anti-Violence Against Women." Violence Against Women 16: 34–60. doi:10.1177/1077801210376749.

Casey, E., and K. Ohler. 2011. "Being a Positive Bystander: Male Antiviolence Allies' Experiences of Stepping Up." Journal Interpersonal Violence 62: 101–19. doi:10.1177/0886260511416479.

Cerulli, C., E. Edwardsen, J. Duda, K. Conner, and E. Caine. 2010. "Protection Order Petitioner's Health Care Utilization." Violence Against Women 16: 679–90. doi:10.1177/1077801210370028.

Center for Disease Control. 2011. "Costs of Intimate Partner Violence Against Women in the United States." http://www.cdc.gov.

Chang, J. C., P. A. Cluss, J. G. Burke, L. Hawker, D. Dado, S. Goldstrohm, and S. H. Scholle, 2011. "Partner Violence Screening in Mental Health." General Hospital Psychiatry 33: 58–65. doi:10.1016/j.genhosppsych.2010.11.009.

Cerulli, C., E. Poleshuck, C. Raimondi, S. Veale, and N. Chin. 2012. "Fresh Hell Is This? Victims of Intimate Partner Violence Describe Their Experiences of Abuse, Pain, and

Depression." *Journal Family Violence* 27: 773–81. doi:10.1007/s10896-012-9469-6.

Collins, J. 2011. "Strategy of Career Interventions for Battered Women." *Human Resource Development Review* 10: 246–63. doi:10.1177/1534484311408691.

Colvin, M., F. Cullen, and V. Ven. 2002. "Coercion, Social Support, and Crime: An Emerging Theoretical Consensus." *Criminology* 40: 19–42. doi:10.1111/j.1745-9125.2002.tb00948.x.

Cramer, E. and S. Brady. 2013. "Competing Values in Serving Older and Vulnerable Adults: Adult Protective Services Mandated Reporting, and Domestic Violence Programs." *Journal of Elder Abuse and Neglect* 25: 453–68. doi:10.1080/08946566.2013.782781.

Corporate Alliance to End Partner Violence. 2013. www.caepv.org.

Cronholm K., S. Bates, N. Nguyen, A. Leahy, M. Blanchard, and K. R. Lentine. 2011. "Validation of a Microbiological Method Using Acholeplasma laidlawii for Assessing Performance of Microporous Membranes for Mycoplasma Clearance." *PDA Journal of Pharmaceutical Science and Technology* 63: 438–61.

Crowne, S. S., M. H. Biar-Merritt, D. A. Thompson, E. Sibinga, M. Trent, and J. Campbell. 2010. "Why Do Women Use Intimate Partner Violence? A Systematic Review of Women's Motivations." *Trauma, Violence, and Abuse* 9: 112–41. doi:10.1177/1524838010379003.

Curwood S. E., I. DeGeer, P. Hymmen, and P. Lehmann. 2011. "Using Strength-Based Approaches to Explore Pretreatment Change in Men Who Abuse Their Partners." *Journal of Interpersonal Violence* 13: 2698–715. doi:10.1177/0886260510388283.

Dai, H. 2013. "To Build an Extended Family: Feminist Organizational Design and Its Dilemmas in Women-Led Non-Governmental

Elder Homes in China." *Social Forces* 92: 1115–34. doi:10.1093/sf/sot103.

Dalal, K., J. Andrews, and S. Dawad. 2012. "Concentration Use and Associations with Intimate Partner Violence Among Women in Bangladesh." *Journal of Biosocial Science* 44: 83–94. doi:10.1017/S0021932011000307.

D'Cruz, P. and E. Noronha. 2011. "The Limits to Workplace Friendship: Managerialist HRM and Bystander Behaviour in the Context of Workplace Bullying." *Employee Relations* 3: 269–88. doi:10.1108/01425451111121777.

Dennis, C., and S. Vigod. 2013. "The Relationship Between Postpartum Depression, Domestic Violence, Childhood Violence, and Substance Use." *Violence against Women* 19: 503–17. doi:10.1177/1077801213487057.

Dennison, S. M., and C. M. Thompson. 2011. "Intimate Partner Violence: The Effect of Gender and Contextual Factors on Community Perceptions of Harm, and Suggested Victim and Criminal Justice Responses." *Violence and Victims* 26: 347–63. doi:10.1891/0886-6708.26.3.347.

Denzin, N. K., and Y. S. Lincoln. 2011. *The Sage Handbook of Qualitative Research*. 4th ed. Thousand Oaks: CA.

Department of Justice. 2012. www.justice.gov.

Devries, K. M., J. Y. Mak, L. J. Bacchus, J. C. Child, G. Falder, M. Petzold, J. Astbury, and C. H. Watts. 2013. "Intimate Partner Violence and Incident Depressive Symptoms and Suicide Attempts: A Systematic Review of Longitudinal Studies." *PLoS Medicine* 10: 1–19. doi:10.1371/journal.pmed.1001439.

Dillona, B. 2012. "Workplace Violence: Impact, Causes, and Prevention." *Work* 42: 15–20. doi:10.3233/WOR-2012-1322.

Exum, M., J. Hartman, P. Friday, and V. Lord. 2010. "Policing Domestic Violence in the Post-SARP Era: The Impact of a

Domestic Violence Police Unit." *Crime and Delinquency* 59, no. 13: 450–63. doi:10.1177/0011128710382345.

Francis, J. J., M. Johnston, C. Robertson, L. Glidewell, V. Entwistle, M. P. Eccles, and J. M. Grimshaw. 2012. "What Is an Adequate Sample Size? Operationalizing Data Saturation for Theory-Based Interview Studies." *Psychology and Health* 25: 1229–45. doi:10.1080/08870440903194015.

Friend, J., J. Langhinrichsen-Rohling, and B. Eichold. 2011. "Same-Day Substance Use in Men and Women Charged with Felony Domestic Violence Offenses." *Criminal Justice and Behavior* 38: 619–33. doi:10.1177/0093854811402768.

Futures Without Violence. 2014. www.futureswithoutviolence.org.

Gauthier, S. 2010. "The Perceptions of Judicial and Psychosocial Interveners of the Consequences of Dropped Charges in Domestic Violence Cases." *Violence Against Women* 16: 1375–95. doi:10.1177/1077801210389163.

General Duty Clause of the OSH Act. 1970. https://www.osha.gov.

Gephart, R. 2004. "From the Editors: Qualitative Research and the Academy of Management Journal." *Academy of Management Journal* 47: 454–62. doi:10.5465/AMJ.2004.14438580.

Glaser, B., and A. Strauss. 1967. *The Discovery of Grounded Theory: Strategies for Qualitative Research.* Chicago, IL: Aline.

Golder, S., and T. Logan. 2010. "Lifetime Victimization and Psychological Distress: Cluster Profiles of Out of Treatment Drug-Involved Women." *Violence and Victims* 25: 62–83. doi:10.1891/0886-6708.25.1.62.

Gotlib, I. and J. Joormann. 2010. "Cognition and Depression: Current Status and Future Directions." *Annual Review of Clinical Psychology* 6: 285–312. doi:10.1146/annurev.clinpsy.121208.131305.

Guoping, H., Z. Yalin, C. Yuping, S. Momartin, and W. Ming. 2010. "Relationship Between Recent Life Events, Social Supports, and Attitudes to Domestic Violence." *Journal of Interpersonal Violence* 25: 863–76. doi:10.1177/0886260509336959.

Hanson, R., G. Sawyer, A. Begle, and G. Hubel. 2010. "The Impact of Crime Victimization on Quality of Life." *Journal of Traumatic Stress* 23: 189–97. doi:10.1002/jts.20508.

Harper, M. and P. Cole. 2012. "Member Checking: Can Benefits Be Gained Similar to Group Therapy?" *Qualitative Report* 17: 510–17. http://www.nova.edu/ssss/QR.

Hartley, C. C., L. M. Renner, and S. Mackel. 2013. "Civil Legal Services and Domestic Violence: Missed Service Opportunities." *Journal Families in Society: The Journal of Contemporary Social Services* 94: 15–22. doi:10.1606/1044-3894.4260.

Harvie, P., and T. Manzi. 2011. "Interpreting Multi-Agency Partnerships: Ideology, Discourse and Domestic Violence." *Social Legal Studies* 20: 79–95. doi:10.1177/0964663910384907.

Hazel, S. 2013. "I Couldn't Even Dress the Way I Wanted. Young Women Talk of 'Ownership' by Boyfriends: An Opportunity for the Prevention of Domestic Violence." *Feminism Psychology* 23: 536–55. doi:10.1177/0959353513481955.

Healey, L., C. Humphreys, and K. Howe. 2013. "Inclusive Domestic Violence Standards: Strategies to Improve Interventions for Women with Disabilities." *Violence and Victims* 28: 50–68. doi:10.1891/0886-6708.28.1.50.

Hearn, J. 2012. "The Sociological Significance of Domestic Violence: Tensions, Paradoxes and Implications." *Current Sociology* 1: 152–70. doi:10.1177/0011392112456503.

Hearn, J. and L. McKie. 2010. "Gendered and Social Hierarchies in Problem Representation and Policy Processes: 'Domestic Violence' in Finland and Scotland." *Violence Against Women* 16: 136–58. doi:10.1177/1077801209355185.

Hellmuth, J. C., V. Jaquier, K. Young-Wolff, and T. P. Sullivan. 2013. "Posttraumatic Stress Disorder Symptom Clusters, Alcohol Misuse, and Women's Use of Intimate Partner Violence." *Journal Traumatic Stress* 26: 451–8. doi:10.1002/jts.21829.

Hester, M. 2011. "The Three Planet Model: Towards an Understanding of Contradictions in Approaches to Women and Children's Safety in Contexts of Domestic Violence." *British Journal of Social Work* 41: 837–53. doi:10.1093/bjsw/bcr095.

Hilton, N., G. Harris, S. Popham, and C. Lang. 2010. "Risk Assessment Among Incarcerated Male Domestic Violence Offenders." *Criminal Justice and Behavior* 37: 815–32. doi:10.1177/0093854810368937.

Hobday, M. 2010. "Domestic Violence Comes to Work: The Need for a Work-Related Response." *Bench and Bar* 67: 19–27. http://mnbenchbar.com.

Howard, J. and B. Wech. 2012. "A Model of Organizational and Job Environment Influences on Workplace Violence." *Employment Responsible Rights Journal* 24: 111–27. doi:10.1007/s10672-011-9181-3.

Iverson, K., S. Litwack, S. Pineles, M. Suvak, R. Vaughn, and P. Resick. 2013. "Predictors of Intimate Partner Violence Revictimization: The Relative Impact of Distinct PTSD Symptoms, Dissociation, and Coping Strategies." *Journal of Traumatic Stress* 26: 102–10. doi:10.1002/jts.21781.

Jewell, L. and J. Wormith. 2010. "Variables Associated with Attrition from Domestic Violence Treatment Programs Targeting Male Batterers." *Criminal Justice and Behavior* 37: 1086–113. doi:10.1177/0093854810376815.

Judge, K., R. Hiscock, and L. Bauld. 2010. "Social Inequalities in Quitting Smoking: What Factors Mediate the Relationship

Between Socioeconomic Position and Smoking Cessation?" *Journal of Public Health* 97.

Keelty, T. 2013. "Shooter in the Workplace: Workplace Violence Planning." *American Society of Safety Engineers* 12: 24–6. http://www.asse.org.

Kelly, U. 2010. "Intimate Partner Violence, Physical Health, Posttraumatic Stress Disorder, Depression, and Quality of Life in Latinas West." *Journal Emergency Medicine* 11: 247–51. doi:PMC2941361.

Kitterlin, M. 2010. "Illegal Substance Abuse in the Full-Service Restaurant Industry: An Evaluation of Pre-Employment Drug-Testing." PhD diss. http://digitalscholarship.unlv.edu/thesesdissertations/241.

Komro, K., R. O'Mara, and A. Wagenaar. 2012. "Mechanisms of Legal Effect: Perspectives from Public Health." *Public Health Law Research Methods Monograph Series.* Advanced online publication. http://www.ssrn.com/en/.

Kulkarni, S. J., H. Bell, and D. M. Rhodes. 2012. "Back to Basics: Essential Qualities of Services for Survivors of Intimate Partner Violence." *Violence Against Women* 18: 85–101.

Kwako, L., J. Noll, F. Putnam, and P. Trickett. 2010. "Childhood Sexual Abuse and Attachment: An Intergenerational Perspective." *Clinical Child Psychology Psychiatry* 15: 407–22. doi:10.1177/1359104510367590.

Kwesiga, E., M. P. Bell, M. Pattie, and A. M. Moe. 2007. "Exploring the Literature on Relationships Between Gender Roles, Intimate Partner Violence Occupational Status, and Organizational Benefits." *Journal of Interpersonal Violence* 22: 312–26. doi:10.1177/0886260506295381.

Labriola, M., S. O'Sullivan, and M. Rempel. 2010. "Court Responses to Batterer Program Non-Compliance: A National Survey." *Judicature* 94: 71–94.

Levendoskya, A., G. Bogata, A. Huth-Bocksb, K. Rosenblumc, and A. Eyea. 2011. "The Effects of Domestic Violence on the Stability of Attachment from Infancy to Preschool. *Journal of Clinical Child and Adolescent Psychology* 40: 398–410. doi:10.1080/15374416.2011.563460.

Lindquist C., T. McKay, M. Clinton-Sherrod, K. M. Pollack, B. Lasater, X. Hardison, and J. Walters. 2010. "The Role of Employee Assistance Programs in Workplace-Based Intimate Partner Violence Intervention and Prevention Activities." *Journal of Workplace Behavioral Health* 25: 46–64. doi:10.1080/15555240903538980.

Livingston, W. 2012. "Group Work with Populations At Risk." *Journal of Social Work* 12: 563–4. doi:10.1300/J497v77n01_07.

Lorsch, J. W. 2010. *A Contingency Theory of Leadership.* Boston, MA: Harvard Business Press.

Macy, R. and M. Goodbourn. 2012. "Promoting Successful Collaborations: Between Domestic Violence and Substance Abuse Treatment Service Sectors." *Trauma Violence Abuse* 13. 234–51. doi:10.1177/1524838012455874.

Macy, R., N. Johns, C. Rizo, S. Martin, and M. Giattina. 2011. "Domestic Violence and Sexual Assault Service Goal Priorities." *Journal of Interpersonal Violence* 26: 3361–82. doi:10.1177/0886260510393003.

Marshall, C. and G. Rossman. 2011. *Designing Qualitative Research.* 5th ed. Thousand Oaks, CA: Sage.

Mdanda, S. 2010. "Exploring a Group of African Male Students' Talk on Gender Equality." *Violence* 23: 343–51. doi:10.1007/s10896-008-9157-8.

Mburia-Mwalili, A., K. Clements-Nolle, W. Lee, M. Shadley, and W. Yang. 2010. "Attachment and Sexual Health Behaviors in Homeless Youth." *Journal for Specialists in Pediatric Nursing* 12: 37–48. doi:10.1111/j.1744-6155.2007.00087.x.

Moola, F., C. Fusco, and J. A. Kirsh. 2011. "The Perceptions of Caregivers Toward Physical Activity and Health in Youth with Congenital Heart Disease." *Qualitative Health Research* 21: 278–91.doi:1049732310384119v1.

Moore, A., L. Frohwirtha, and E. Miller. 2010. "Male Reproductive Control of Women Who Have Experienced Intimate Partner Violence in the United States." *Social Science and Medicine* 70: 1737–44. doi:10.1016/j.socscimed.2010.02.009.

Murray, C., and M. Welch. 2010. "Preliminary Construction of a Service Provider: Informed Domestic Violence Research Agenda." *Journal Interpersonal Violence* 25: 2279–96. doi:10.1177/0886260509354883.

Nichols, A. 2011. "Gendered Organizations: Challenges for Domestic Violence Victim Advocates and Feminist Advocacy." *Feminist Criminology* 6, no. 2: 111–31. doi:10.1177/1557085111398117.

Nelson, E. 2012. "Police Controlled Antecedents Which Significantly Elevate Prosecution and Conviction Rates in Domestic Violence Cases." *Criminology and Criminal Justice* 13: 526–51. doi:10.1177/1748895812462594.

Nurius, P., P. Logan-Greene, and S. Green. 2012. ACEs Within a Social Disadvantage Framework: Distinguishing, Unique, Cumulative, and Moderated Contributions to Adult Mental Health." *Journal Prev Interv Community* 40: 278–90. doi:10.10 80/10852352.2012.707443.

Nurius, P. S., R. J. Macy, I. Nabuzor, and V. L. Holt. 2011. "Intimate Partner Survivors' Help-Seeking and Protection Efforts: A

Person-Oriented Analysis. *Journal of Interpersonal Violence* 26: 539–66. doi:10.1177/0886260510363422.

Oaksforda, M. and N. Chatera. 2009. "Précis of Bayesian Rationality: The Probabilistic Approach to Human Reasoning." *Behavioral and Brain Sciences* 32. 69–84. doi:10.1017/S0140525X09000284.

Pallitto, C., C. García-Moreno, H. Jansen, L. Heise, M. Ellsberg, and C. Watts. 2013. "Intimate Partner Violence, Abortion, and Unintended Pregnancy: Results from the WHO Multi-Country Study on Women's Health and Domestic Violence." *International Journal of Gynecology and Obstetrics* 120: 3–9. doi:10.1016/j.ijgo.2012.07.003.

Park, J. 2011. "Retirement, Health and Employment Among Those 55 Plus." Statistics Canada.

Patton, M. Q. 2002. *Qualitative Research and Evaluation Methods*. Thousand Oaks, CA: Sage Publications.

Perrin, N., N. Yragui, G. Hanson, and N. Glass. 2011. "Patterns of Workplace Supervisor Support Desired by Abused Women." *Journal of Interpersonal Violence* 26: 2264–84. doi:10.1177/0886260510383025.

Pollack, K., W. Austin, and J. Grisso. 2010. "Employee Assistance Programs: A Workplace Resource to Address Intimate Partner Violence." *Journal of Women's Health* 19: 729–33. doi:10.1089/jwh.2009.1495.

Pollet, S. 2005. "Domestic Violence in the Workplace: It's an Employer's Business." *Employment Law, Strategist*. 1–5. http://www.ncdsv.org.

Potter, S., and V. Banyard. 2011. "The Victimization Experiences of Women in the Workforce: Moving Beyond Single Categories of Work or Violence." *Violence and Victims* 26: 513–32. doi:10.1891/0886-6708.26.4.513.

Powers, R. and S. Simpson. 2012. "Self-Protective Behaviors and Injury in Domestic Violence Situations: Does It Hurt to Fight Back?" *Journal of Interpersonal Violence* 27: 3345–65. doi:10.1177/0886260512445384.

Puccia, E., T. Redding, R. Brown, R. Gwynne, A. Hirsh, R. Hoffmann, and B. Morrison. 2012. "Using Community Outreach and Evidenced-Based Treatment to Address Domestic Violence Issues." *Social Work in Mental Health* 10: 104–26. doi:10.1080/15332985.2011.601704.

Reeves, S., J. Goldman, J. Gilbert, J. Tepper, I. Silver, E. Suter, and M. Zwarenstein. 2011. "A Scoping Review to Improve Conceptual Clarity of Interprofessional Interventions." *Journal of Interprofessional Care* 25: 167–74. doi:10.3109/13561820.2014.906391.

Renner, L., and W. Stephen. 2010. "Examining Symmetry in Intimate Partner Violence Among Young Adults Using Socio-Demographic Characteristics." *Journal of Family Violence* 25: 91–106. doi:10.1007/s10896-0099273-0.

Riger, S. and S. Staggs. 2011. "A Nationwide Survey of State-Mandated Evaluation Practices for Domestic Violence Agencies." *Journal of Interpersonal Violence* 26: 50–70. doi:10.1177/0886260510362887.

Rigterink, T., L. Karowlatz, and D. Hessler. 2010. "Domestic Violence and Longitudinal Associations with Children's Physiological Regulation Abilities." *Journal of Interpersonal Violence* 25: 1669–83. doi:10.1177/0886260509354589.

Resnicoff, S. H. 2012. "Jewish Law and the Tragedy of Sexual Abuse of Children—The Dilemma within the Orthodox Jewish Community." *Rutgers Journal of Law and Religion* 13, no. 2: 1–90. http://www.ssrn.com/en.

Rothman E. F., M. R. Decker, E. Miller, E. Reed, A. Raj, and J. G. Silverman. 2011. "Multi-Person Sex Among a Sample of Adolescent Female Urban Health Clinic Patients." *Journal of Urban Health: Bulletin of the New York Academy of Medicine* 89: 129–37. doi:10,1007/s11524-001-96307.

Rubin, H. J. and I. S. Rubin. 2012. *Qualitative Interviewing: The Art of Hearing Data.* 3rd ed. Thousand Oaks, CA: Sage Publications.

Sagor, M. 2012. "When Domestic Violence Comes to Work." http://www.compeap.com.

Schenck-Gustafsson K., P. R. De Cola, D. W. Pfaff, and D. S. Pisetsky. 2012. *Handbook of Clinical Gender Medicine.* 99–124. doi:10.1159/000336382.

Sen, R. 2010. "Women's Subjectivities of Suffering and Legal Rhetoric on Domestic Violence: Fissures in the Two Discourses." *Indian Journal of Gender Studies* 17: 375–401. doi:10.1177/097152151001700304.

Shinkfield, A., and J. Graffam. 2010. "The Relationship Between Emotional State and Success in Community Reintegration for Ex-Prisoners." *International Journal Offender Therapy Comparative Criminology* 5: 346–60. doi:10.1177/0306624X09331443.

Shorey, R., H. Brasfield, J. Febres, and G. Stuart. 2011. "The Association Between Impulsivity Trait Anger and the Perpetration of Intimate Partner and General Violence Among Women Arrested for Domestic Violence." *Journal of Interpersonal Violence* 26: 2681–97. doi:10.1177/0886260510388289.

Shuck, B. 2011. "An Integrative Literature Review: Four Emerging Perspectives of Employee Engagement." *Human Resource Development Review* 10: 304–28. doi:10.1177/1534484311410840.

Simmons, C., M. Farrar, K. Frazer, and M. Thompson. 2011. "From the Voices of Women: Facilitating Survivor Access to IPV Services." *Violence Against Women* 17: 1226–43. doi:10.1177/1077801211424476.

Sohani, Z., H. Shannon, J. W. Busse, D. Tikacz, P. Sancheti, M. Shende, and M. Bhandari. 2013. "Feasibility of Screening for Intimate Partner Violence at Orthopedic Trauma Hospitals in India." *Journal of Interpersonal Violence* 28: 1455–75. doi:10.1177/0886260512468244.

Sullivan, C. 2011. "Evaluating Domestic Violence Support Service Programs: Waste of Time, Necessary Evil, or Opportunity for Growth." *Aggression and Violent Behavior* 16: 354–60. doi:10.1016/j.avb.2011.04.008.

Stake, R.E. 2010. *Qualitative Research: Studying How Things Work*. New York, NY: Guilford Press.

Stark, E. 2010. "Do Violent Acts Equal Abuse? Resolving the Gender Parity/Asymmetry Dilemma." *Sex Roles* 62: 201–11. doi:10.1007/s11199-009-9717-2.

Suneetha, A. and V. Nagaraj. 2010. "Dealing with Domestic Violence Towards Complicating the Rights Discourse." *Indian Journal of Gender Studies* 17: 451–78. doi:10.1177/097152151001700307.

Suri, H. 2011. "Purposeful Sampling in Qualitative Research Synthesis." *Qualitative Research Journal* 11: 63–75. doi:10.3316/QRJ1102063.

Swanberg, J. E., T. K. Logan, and C. Macke. 2006. "Intimate Partner Violence, Employment, and the Workplace: Consequences and Future Directions." *Trauma, Violence, and Abuse* 6: 286–312. doi:10.1177/1524838005280506.

Swanberg, J., M. Ojha, and C. Macke. 2012. "State Employment Protection Statutes for Victims of Domestic Violence: Public Policy's Response to Domestic Violence as an Employment

Matter." *Journal of Interpersonal Violence* 27: 587–619. doi:10.1177/0886260511421668.

Teddlie, C. and F. Yu. 2007. "Mixed Methods Sampling: A Typology with Examples." *Journal of Mixed Methods Research* 2: 81–111. doi:10.1177/2345678906292430.

Tuerkheimer, D. 2013. "Breakups." *Yale Journal of Law and Feminism* 51: 1–49. doi:10.2139/ssrn.1980021.

U.S. Department of Health and Human Services. 2014. *Understanding and Responding to Violence in the Workplace.* http://www.hhs.gov.

Ueno, R., and K. Kamibeppu. 2011. "Relationship Between Positive Self-Recognition of Maternal Role and Psychosocial Factors in Japanese Mothers with Severe Mental Illness." *Community Mental Health Journal* 47: 520–30. doi:10.1007/s10597-010-9344-y.

Valdiserri, G. A., and J. L. Wilson. 2010. "The Study of Leadership in Small Business Organizations: Impact on Profitability and Organizational Success." *The Entrepreneurial Executive* 15: 47–71. http://www.alliedacademies.org.

Usta, J., L. Antoun, B. Ambuel, and M. Khawaja. 2012. "Involving the Health Care System in Domestic Violence: What Women Want." *Annals of Family Medicine* 10: 213–20. doi:10.1370/afm.1336.

Virginia Department of Health. 2013. "Domestic Violence Fatality Review." http://www.vdh.virginia.gov.

Walker, D., C. Neighbors, L. Mbilinyi, A. O'Rourke, J. Zegree, R. Roffman, and J. Edleson. 2010. "Evaluating the Impact of Intimate Partner Violence on the Perpetrator: The Perceived Consequences of Domestic Violence Questionnaire." *Journal of Interpersonal Violence* 25: 1684–98. doi:10.1177/0886260509354592.

Wells, L., J. Emery, C. Herbert, and T. Boodt. 2012. "Preventing Domestic Violence in Alberta: A Cost Savings Perspective." SPP Research Paper No. 12–17. http://dx.doi.org/10.2139/ssrn.2088960.

Whitaker, D., C. Murphy, C. Eckhardt, A. Hodges, and M. Cowart. 2013. "Effectiveness of Primary Prevention Efforts for Intimate Partner Violence." *Partner Abuse* 4: 175–95. doi:10.1891/1946-6560.4.2.175.

Widiss, D. A. 2008. *Domestic Violence and Employment: Towards a Holistic Approach* 35: 669–728. http://diginole.lib.fsu.edu/cgi/viewcontent.cgi? article=1142andcontext=fsulr.

Wies, J. and K. Coy. 2013. "Measuring Violence: Vicarious Trauma Among Sexual Assault Nurse Examiners." *Human Organization* 72: 23–30. http://sfaa.metapress.com/home/main.mpx.

Wilson, H. A., and R. D. Hoge. 2013. "The Effect of Youth Diversion Programs on Recidivism: A Meta-Analytic Review." *Criminal Justice and Behavior* 40: 497–518.

Wisdom, J. P., M. A. Cavaleri, A. J. Onwuegbuzie, and C. A. Green. 2012. "Methodological Reporting in Qualitative, Quantitative, and Mixed Methods Health Services Research Articles." *Health Services Research* 47: 721–45. doi:10.1111/j.1475-6773.2011.01344.

Wong F., J. DiGangi, D. Young, J. Huang, B. Smith, and D. John. 2010. "Intimate Partner Violence, Depression, and Alcohol Use Among a Sample of Foreign-Born Southeast Asian Women in an Urban Setting in the United States." *Journal of Interpersonal Violence* 26: 211–29. doi:10.1177/0886260510362876.

Wu, E., N. El-Bassela, L. Gilberta, B. Sarfoa, and R. Seewald. 2010. "Criminal Justice Involvement and Service Need Among Men on Methadone Who Have Perpetrated Intimate

Partner Violence." *Journal of Criminal Justice* 38: 835–40. doi:10.1016/j.jcrimjus.2010.05.012.

Wu, Y., D. Button, N. Smolter, and M. Poteyeva. 2013. "Public Responses to Intimate Partner Violence: Comparing Preferences of Chinese and American College Students." *Violence and Victims* 28: 303–23. doi:10.1891/0886-6708. VV-D-12-00001.

Wu, V., H. Huff, and M. Bhandari. 2010. "Pattern of Physical Injury Associated with Intimate Partner Violence in Women Presenting to the Emergency Department: A Systematic Review and Meta-Analysis." *Trauma, Violence, Abuse* 1: 71–82. doi:10.1177/1524838010367503.

Yin, R. 2009. *Case Study Research: Designs and Methods*. 4th ed. Thousand Oaks, CA: Sage.

Zalmanowitz, S., R. Babins-Wagner, S. Rodger, B. Corbett, and A. Leschied. 2013. "The Association of Readiness to Change and Motivational Interviewing with Treatment Outcomes in Males Involved in Domestic Violence Group Therapy." *Journal of Interpersonal Violence* 28: 956–74. doi:10.1177/0886260512459381.

Zammuto, R., T. Griffith, A. Majchrzak, D. Dougherty, and S. Fara. 2007. "Information Technology and the Changing Fabric Organization." *Organization Science* 18: 749–62. doi:10.1287/orsc.1070.0307.

Appendix A: Consent Form

You are invited to take part in a research study of what policies and procedures are implemented to help produce an environment that is supportive to victims of externally generated workplace violence and that safeguards the responsibilities of employers. You were chosen for the study because you are a manager with experience in the workplace. This form is part of a process called "informed consent," which allows you to understand this study before deciding whether to join the study. This name of the investigator of this study is Markeith Porter, a doctoral candidate at CALUMS University. The participants are coworkers who have at least a year in industry and who have been deemed a consummate professional.

Background Information:

The purpose of this study is to describe what policies and procedures are implemented to help produce an environment that is supportive to victims of externally generated workplace violence and that safeguards the responsibilities of employers in industry.

Procedures:

If you agree to take part in this study, you must be at least eighteen with at least one year of experience in the field. You will need approximately twenty minutes to complete the questionnaire.

Voluntary Nature of the Study:

Your participation in this study is voluntary. This means that I will respect your decision of whether you want to participant in this research. No one will treat you differently if you decide to withdraw from the study. If you decide to join the study now, you could still change your mind during the study. If you become anxious during the study, you could stop at any time. You could skip any questions that you think are too personal.

Risks and Benefits of Participating in the Study:

The risk involved in the study is minimal, such as fatigue and recalling unpleasant situations. Your identity will remain confidential. The benefit of joining this study includes your contribution to the discourse of externally generated workplace violence in the coastal area of the US Southwest.

Compensation:

No award is granted to those who participate.

Confidentiality:

Any information you provide is kept confidential. The investigator will not use your information for any purposes outside of this research project. In addition, the investigator will not include your name or anything else that could identify you in any reports of the study.

Contacts and Questions:

You could ask any questions you have now. If you have questions later, you could contact the inquirer via phone number and e-mail address.

The investigator will give you a copy of this form to keep.

Statement of Consent:

The examiner will keep my personal information confidential. I certify that information I provide is truthful to the best of my ability. I have read the above information, and I understand the study enough to make a decision about my involvement. By inserting my signature below, I agree to the terms described above.

Printed Name of Participant

Date of Consent

Participant's Written or Electronic* Signature

Researcher's Written or Electronic* Signature

Appendix B: Subquestions and Interview Questions

The following research subquestions and interview questions will help guide the study:

Subquestions
1. What protocols and policies are implemented for the prevention, intervention, and dealing with the aftermath of violence that infiltrates the workplace?
2. What training are managers and employees given about externally generated workplace violence?
3. How could leaders create an environment that supports victims of externally generated workplace violence where these individuals will report potential dangers of violence that could potentially infiltrate the workplace?
4. How could managers create an environment in which perpetrators know that violence is not acceptable behavior (on or off the job), and what community resources are available to offer help in changing behavior?

Interview Questions
1. How long have you been working as a manager in business?
2. How did you construct your policy to manage the issue of externally generated workplace violence?
3. How effective is the current policy and training on externally generated workplace violence?

4. How could regulations or laws help to manage externally generated workplace violence in business?
5. How could multidisciplinary teams (MT) perform in dealing with externally generated workplace violence in business?
6. What roles do each member of the MT play in dealing with externally generated workplace violence issues?
7. What training do supervisors and employees receive about how to respond to suspected externally generated workplace violence?
8. What symptoms are associated with externally generated workplace violence prior to an incident occurring?
9. What intervention and prevention measures are implemented for you as a manager?
10. What procedures and processes are implemented that demonstrate a climate of zero tolerance?
11. What other aspects could you offer to discuss about your company's current policies to prevent and address externally generated workplace violence?

Appendix C: Case Study Protocol

1. Introduction
2. Research Question
3. Conceptual Framework
a. Psychological capital framework (Luthans 2002)
4. Data Collection Procedures
a. Data to be collected from the review of documents and the conduct of semistructured interviews
b. Expected preparation activities to take place prior to conducting interviews
c. Preparation of informed consent forms for each interviewee
d. Review and finalization of planned interview questions
e. Scheduling of conference rooms to conduct interviews
5. Data Collection Tools
a. Digital audio recordings
b. Researcher field notes
c. Case study database
6. Data Analysis Techniques and Tools
a. Inductive coding
b. Analysis tools
c. ATLAS.ti
7. Study Credibility and Dependability Methods
a. Credibility method
b. Multiple data sources (construct validity)

c. Assessment of rival explanations, research bias identification, peer debriefing, member checking, and transcript checking (internal validity)
d. Rich description of study sample population (external validity)
8. Dependability methods
a. Case study protocol use
b. Case study database creation
9. Procedural Guide
a. Overview of study
b. Presentation of the findings
c. Applications to professional practice
d. Implications for social change
e. Recommendations for action
f. Recommendations for further study
g. Reflections
h. Summary and study conclusions

Curriculum Vitae

Markeith Porter

SUMMARY: Extensive military experience involving leadership, maintenance management, equipment maintenance, equipment operation, systems testing, curriculum development, and training.
EXPERTISE: Project management, systems administration, training, supervision, database administration, troubleshooting, personnel development, team building, electrical safety, coaching, planning, quality assurance, resource management, budgeting, technical writing
OBJECTIVE: To obtain a job in middle management or above
EXPERIENCE: U. S. Navy, Chief Fire Controlman/Electronics Technician, 12/2009 to Present BAE SYSTEMS Ship Superintendent

- Technical skills: ability to understand contracts, business law, and Federal Acquisition Regulations (FAR).
- Financial skills: knowledge of cost accounting principles and to produce financial analysis models using various software programs, such as Deltek and Costpoint.
- Leadership: manage multimillion-dollar production and manufacturing projects using Earned Value Management System principles.
- Oversee the execution and completion of production and repair solutions projects in the production arena.
- Manage resources assigned to projects supporting company-client relationship, ensuring customer satisfaction.

- Provide budget analysis, labor planning, and coordination of activities between client and company personnel.
- Monitor project completion from initiation through delivery to meet revenue and cost projections.
- Oversee the performance of the installation and client acceptance of capitalized equipment, enterprise software systems, or system integration projects or engagements.
- Apply management and technical skills.
- Serve as mediator to internal issues and conflicting priorities for members of cross-functional teams focused on the delivery of new or existing products to clients

Pinkerton Government Services, Site Manager, 12/2006–12/2009
- Wrote Post Orders for security stations for various positions, which included proposals for work acceptance to capture new business.
- Managed a team of thirty-nine security officers to successful acceptance of two renewals of the contract.
- Prepared solicitation documents (RFQ, RFP), equipment specifications and contracts

Systems Test Officer and Maintenance and Course Manager, 08/1984–2006.
- As a Senior Enlisted staff member, developed scenarios using various training experience and configuration and operation experience for the following systems: Modeling and Simulation, Battle Force Team Trainer (BFTT); Tactical Data Information Link generation systems supporting LOS Link 11(A) /16(J); Link 16, Global Command and Control System-Maritime (GCCS-M); Tactical Voice/Data Communications.

- Coordinated preventive and corrective maintenance, systems integration, and testing for shipboard and aviation electronics weapons and support systems to include C4I computer systems.
- As team manager, led the cross-functional team in troubleshooting efforts.
- Led six different courses to 97 percent graduation rate, while dealing with several distracting issues. Obtained a Master Training designation while instructing at Fleet Training Center San Diego, which qualified me to teach any subject using Task Base and Performance Base Instructing techniques.
- Managed the recruitment, development, and training of recruitment staff.
- Led a medical staff that consisted of three doctors, two operating rooms, a dental facility, and pharmacy. Received the Black H for maintaining the highest medical standards.
- Acted as database coordinator for Federal Volunteer Income Tax Program. Created more than ten thousand tax returns, saving government personnel more than five million dollars in tax preparation fees.
- Managed company network, provided troubleshooting for customers, and ensured efficiency of company-wide computer operations. Novelist experience in systems programming, analysis, and data administration services. Communicated with clients to ensure end-user information discrepancies resolved.
- Created Tables for Structured Query Language (SQL) relational database. Conducted queries both simple and complex and deleted tables. Created privileges and revoked privileges. Performed database security support requirements and

performed database monitoring and tuning along with system backups.
- Managed fifty-two technicians in the preventive and corrective maintenance of six electronic weapons systems.
- Served as technical liaison between training executives and training personnel, coordinating course convenings, instructor training, and equipment maintenance. Successfully implemented organizational policy.
- Acted as Configuration Program Manager for several platforms, in which I coordinated software and hardware configurations for several weapons and computer support systems.
- Performed aspects of Quality Assurance to include electronic measurement using various measuring devices. Performed various pressure tests, leak tests, dynamic tests, static tests, and hydrostatic tests.
- Performed aspects of the supply chain to include requisition, procurement, part receipt processing, shipping, and tech editing. Performed aspects of integrated logistics processes to include inventory auditing and surveying parts and HAZMAT. Processed 1149 shipping receipts and 1250s. Worked with numerous supply databases and performed fault analysis on various computer network systems. Worked with vendors to ensure part delivery for scheduled deadlines. Processed parts using bar code readers and labeled and marked inventory. Prepared solicitation documents (RFQ, RFP), equipment specifications, and contracts.
- Managed the handling and transportation of the finished product from the time it left the production line until it reached the customer's location. Shipped, packaged, order picked domestic and international documentation and transportation forms. Supervised the timely communication with production

and transportation companies to ensure orders arrived at the customer's location without any trouble and on time.
- Developed and implemented process improvements in the internal areas of logistics. Managed the department budget, making capital purchases while hiring, training, and disciplining employees.
- Wrote budget proposals, periodic reports, performance evaluation, and award recommendations.
- Awarded the Navy Commendation Medal for strong leadership and management abilities.

EDUCATION:
- Associate of Science in Electronics, New York Regents, Albany, NY
- Bachelor of Science in Information Technology, University of Phoenix, San Diego, CA
- Master's in Business Administration, University of Phoenix, San Diego, CA

COMPUTER SKILLS:
PC, Word, Outlook, PowerPoint, Access, SQL, Oracle, Excel, C++, Visual Basic, Microsoft Project, Internet, Software Engineering and the ability to use Enterprise Resource Programs such as SAP.

QUALIFICATIONS:
Department of Labor Journeymen Electronics Mechanic, Quality Assurance Inspector, Technical Training Instructor, Master Training Specialist, Total Quality Management. Lean Six Sigma.

CLEARANCE:
Secret

www.ingramcontent.com/pod-product-compliance
Lightning Source LLC
Chambersburg PA
CBHW051720170526
45167CB00002B/729